Houghton Mifflin
Math

CHAPTER Challenges

GRADE **4**

- For mathematically promising students

- Opportunities to explore, extend, and connect mathematical ideas

 HOUGHTON MIFFLIN

BOSTON

A Note to the Teacher

According to the *Principles and Standards for School Mathematics,* "All students need access to a coherent, challenging mathematic curriculum."

In the monograph *Activating Mathematical Talent,* the editors stress "the importance of recognizing and activating promising students' mathematical talent." According to their research, activities that foster critical thinking and reasoning skills meet the following criteria:

▶ Problems should go beyond routine classroom exercises.

▶ Problems should be interesting, tantalizing, and engaging.

▶ Creativity should take precedence over prior knowledge or mathematical training.

▶ Different approaches to each problem should be tried, discussed, and evaluated.

In order to engage the mathematical talents of all of our students it is necessary to continually provide a variety of activities that allow students to explore, extend, and connect the mathematical concepts and relationships presented in each chapter. Many students will frequently find these Chapter Challenges interesting and supportive of the learning objectives of the chapter.

Some students will consistently turn to Chapter Challenges as a resource for more stimulating problems and a deeper understanding of the mathematics. These so-called "promising mathematical students" will benefit most from Chapter Challenges.

Nevertheless, because we cannot always identify which students will successfully complete a given chapter challenge, it is important to expose *all* students to these more challenging contexts. As a result, Chapter Challenges provides promising mathematical students with consistent exposure to higher-level thinking situations while providing all students access to mathematical enrichments.

Principles and Standards for School Mathematics, (2000) National Council of Teachers of Mathematics.

Vogali, Bruce R. and Alexander Karp, Editors, (2003) *Activating Mathematical Talent,* NCSM Monograph Series, Volume 1.

Contents

Contents

Name _____ Date _____

Number Names

Everyday you use numbers to count things. The names of some very large numbers and what those numbers look like are shown here.

A million is written with 6 zeros: 1,000,000.
A million is actually 10 × 10 × 10 × 10 × 10 × 10.
Notice that the number 10 is used as a factor
6 times, so there are 6 zeros in 1,000,000.
A billion is written with 9 zeros: 1,000,000,000.
A trillion is written with 12 zeros: 1,000,000,000,000.

> **Remember**
> Factors are the numbers you multiply to find a product.

Do you see a pattern? Continue the pattern to write these numbers.

1. A quadrillion is written with _____ zeros: _____.

2. A quintillion is written with _____ zeros: _____.

3. A sextillion is written with _____ zeros: _____.

4. A septillion is written with _____ zeros: _____.

5. An octillion is written with _____ zeros: _____.

6. A nonillion is written with _____ zeros: _____.

7. A decillion is written with _____ zeros: _____.

An even greater number is called a googol. A googol is a 1 with 100 zeros after it. That's a lot of zeros!

8. Analyze Do you think that there is a greatest number? _____

Explain. _____

_____

Explore It

Suppose it takes you about 1 second to write each digit in a number. On a separate sheet of paper, estimate how long it would take you to write a googol. Check your estimate by writing a googol.

Teacher Notes

Explore: Number Names

Objective Explore names for large numbers.

Using the Explore (Activities to use after Lesson 2)
In this activity, students learn the names of very large numbers. They explore a pattern that occurs as these numbers increase. Then students continue this pattern to write even greater numbers. The critical thinking question introduces students to the concept of infinity. The Explore It helps students begin to get some idea of the size of a googol.

Math Journal You may wish to have students use their *Math Journals* to answer the Explore It question.

Going Beyond Have students guess what a googolplex is and tell how it relates to a googol. The googolplex is a specific finite number. A googolplex is 1 followed by a googol of zeros.

Students might get some idea of the size of this very large number from the fact that there would not be enough room to write it, if they went to the farthest star, touring all the nebulae and putting down zeros every inch of the way.

Solutions

9; 9
12; 12

1. A quadrillion is written with 15 zeros: 1,000,000,000,000,000.

2. A quintillion is written with 18 zeros: 1,000,000,000,000,000,000.

3. A sextillion is written with 21 zeros: 1,000,000,000,000,000,000,000.

4. A septillion is written with 24 zeros: 1,000,000,000,000,000,000,000,000.

5. An octillion is written with 27 zeros: 1,000,000,000,000,000,000,000,000,000.

6. A nonillion is written with 30 zeros: 1,000,000,000,000,000,000,000,000,000,000.

7. A decillion is written with 33 zeros: 1,000,000,000,000,000,000,000,000,000,000,000.

8. *Answers may vary. Sample:* No. You can always count one more. Some students might refer to infinity.

Explore It It would take about 101 seconds, or 1 minute 41 seconds, to write a googol.

Say It with Exponents

You can write greater numbers in different forms.
Standard form: 2,345
Expanded form: $(2 \times 1,000) + (3 \times 100) + (4 \times 10) + (5 \times 1)$.

These products can also be
written as powers of ten.
$1,000 = 10 \times 10 \times 10$
$100 = 10 \times 10$

You can use exponents
to show the powers of 10.
$1,000 = 10 \times 10 \times 10 = 10^3$.
$100 = 10 \times 10 = 10^2$

In the number 10^3, 10 is the base and 3 is the exponent.
The base, 10, is the factor that is repeated. The exponent,
3, is the number of times the base is used as a factor.

You can use powers of ten and exponents to write numbers
in expanded form. Let's look again at the number 2,345.
Expanded form: $(2 \times 1,000) + (3 \times 100) + (4 \times 10) + (5 \times 1)$.
Expanded form with exponent: $(2 \times 10^3) + (3 \times 10^2) + (4 \times 10^1) + (5 \times 10^0)$.

Use exponents to write each number in expanded form.

1. 446 ——————————————————————————————————————

2. 5,397 ————————————————————————————————————

3. 15,704 ——————————————————————————————————

4. Compare Which is greater: $(9 \times 10^3) + (8 \times 10^2)$ or $(2 \times 10^6) + (1 \times 10^2)$?

Explain. Hint: Look at the exponents first! ——————————————————

Extend It

How can you use the number of zeros in 10,000 to help you write this
number using exponents? Does your method work for other powers of ten?

Teacher Notes

Extend: Say It with Exponents

Objective Use exponents to write a number in expanded form.

Using the Extend (Activities to use after Lesson 3)

In this activity, students adept at writing numbers in expanded form try their hand at including the use of exponents. The critical thinking question tests students' understanding of the concept. The Extend It helps students relate the number of zeros in the power of ten to the exponent.

Math Journal You may wish to have students use their *Math Journals* to answer the Extend It question.

Going Beyond Have students write numbers through hundred millions in expanded form using exponents.

Solutions

1. $(4 \times 10^2) + (4 \times 10^1) + (6 \times 10^0)$

2. $(5 \times 10^3) + (3 \times 10^2) + (9 \times 10^1) + (7 \times 10^0)$

3. $(1 \times 10^4) + (5 \times 10^3) + (7 \times 10^2) + (0 \times 10^1) + (4 \times 10^0)$

4. $(2 \times 10^6) + (1 \times 10^2)$ is greater. *Explanations may vary. Sample:* By looking at the first exponent, 6, you know that this number is in the millions. The first exponent in the other number is a 3, so that number is in the thousands.

Extend It *Answers may vary. Sample:* There are 4 zeros in 10,000, and the exponent is 4. Yes. This method works for other powers of ten.

Name _____ Date _____

Quipu

The Incas lived in South America around 1500. They used knotted cords to record numbers of objects they counted. The types of knots and their position on the cords represented the numbers. They called this device a **quipu**.

Some quipus were very elaborate and had many cords branching off in different directions.

Look at the drawing of a quipu below. It shows the positions of the knots. First look at the cords. Then look at the knots and the spaces between them. The first two cords are labeled with the numbers they represent.

Explore the system by studying the labeled cords. Then label the rest of the cords with the numbers they represent.

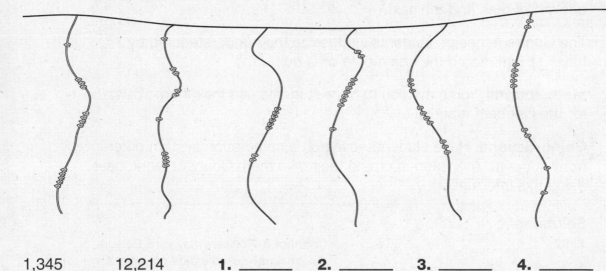

1,345   12,214   **1.** _____ **2.** _____ **3.** _____ **4.** _____

5. **Compare and Contrast** What do you notice about the numbers

when the knots start high up on the cords? _____

Connect It

Count different categories of objects in the classroom or at home. Then make a quipu of your own. Draw the cords and knots. Use a different color for each category of object you are counting.

Teacher Notes

Connect: Quipu

Objective Read and record numbers on a quipu.
Materials colored pencils

Using the Connect (Activities to use after Lesson 5)

In this activity, students examine how the Incas calculated numbers on a device called a **quipu**. The knots were tied in the cords to represent units of ten and multiples of ten according to where they were placed.

The critical thinking question asks students to think about the position of the knots on the cord. The closer to the top the knot was placed, the greater the number, and vice versa. A knot at the top of the cord represented the highest number, 10,000. A knot at the bottom represented ones. The cord had to be long enough for 9 knots between one set of tens and the next.

The Connect It helps students synthesize their understanding by having them record their own data on a quipu.

Math Journal You may wish to have students use their *Math Journals* for the Connect It activity.

Going Beyond Have students research a numeration system different from our own. Ask them to create their own math Connect worksheet using this information.

Solutions

1. 62

2. 2,710

3. 343

4. 25,211

5. The numbers are greater when the knots start higher up on the cords. You might point out to students that the closer the knot is placed to the top the higher the number and vice versa.

Connect It *Answers may vary.* Be sure students have used a different color for each category. Then check the position and numbers of the knots they made.

What's Wrong?

A car dealer made this chart to show the number of yearly car sales in the U.S. from 1990 to 2000. He asked his assistant to check the numbers. Here's what she reported.

In 1990, there were actually 10,000 more sales than the number in the chart. In 1992, there were 1,000,000 more sales. In 1993, there were 10 fewer sales. In 1996, there were 100,000 fewer sales. In 1998, there were 1,000 fewer sales. In 2000, there were 100 more sales.

Write the correct number of car sales in the spaces provided in the chart.

1990	9,290,211	1996	8,626,753
1. _____		**4.** _____	
1991	8,174,656	1997	8,272,074
1992	7,213,112	1998	8,142,721
2. _____		**5.** _____	
1993	8,517,869	1999	8,698,284
3. _____			
1994	8,990,517	2000	8,846,525
		6. _____	
1995	8,634,964		

7. The year with the greatest number of sales was _____.

   The year with the least number of sales was _____.

8. During which years were sales greater than 8,750,000?

   _____

9. During which years were sales less than 8,500,000?

   _____

10. **Analyze** During which years were sales greater

    than 8,500,000 and less than 8,800,000? _____

Explore It

What happened to car sales during the ten-year period? Did they increase every year? Did they decrease? What kind of display could the car dealer make to show how the sales changed over the years?

Teacher Notes

Explore: What's Wrong?

Objective Compare numbers to analyze data.

Using the Explore (Activities to use after Lesson 1)

In this activity, students apply their skills with place value, comparing numbers, and analyzing data. They provide and identify pieces of data that satisfy certain criteria. The Analyze question requires that the students use critical thinking to find numbers that fall between two other numbers. In Explore It, students may recognize that making a line graph or a bar graph is a way to show data that changes over time.

Math Journal You may wish to have students use their *Math Journals* to answer the Explore It question.

Going Beyond In Explore It, students are asked to think about different ways to display data. You may want to have them cut out examples of different types of graphs from newspapers and magazines.

Solutions

1. 9,300,211
2. 8,213,112
3. 8,517,859
4. 8,526,753
5. 8,141,721
6. 8,846,625
7. 1990; 1998
8. 1990, 1994, 2000
9. 1991, 1992, 1997, 1998
10. 1993, 1995, 1996, 1999

Explore It Sales went down, then up, then down, and then up again. There was no pattern in the increase or decrease of sales. Either a line graph or a bar graph would be a good way to show how sales changed over time.

Invention Timeline

This chart lists inventions and the years they were invented. These inventions are listed in alphabetical order. To show them in the order in which they were invented, you would create a timeline.

Invention	Date
Color television	1928
Mason jar	1858
Mini van	1983
Paper clip	1900
Piano	1709
Safety pin	1849
Seat belt	1959
Velcro	1948
Video game	1972

A timeline shows events in order according to when the events occurred. A timeline is a type of number line. The numbers on a timeline are dates—usually years. A timeline can be a horizontal line or a vertical line. A horizontal timeline, like the one below, shows the dates starting from the earliest date, on the left, to the latest date, on the right.

1. Use the data in the chart above. Put the inventions in order, based on the years they were invented. Start with the earliest invention. Then place the date and the name of the invention on the timeline.

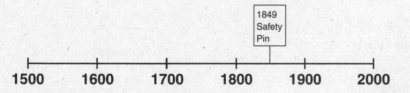

```
       1849
       Safety
       Pin
├────┼────┼────┼────┼────┼────┼
1500  1600  1700  1800  1900  2000
```

2. Here are more dates of inventions. Show these dates on your timeline.

    1979 1777 1608 1885 1972 1589 1903

3. **Decide** Here is a list of the inventions that belong to the dates in Exercise 2: automobile, compact disc, windshield wiper, circular saw, flush toilet, compact disc player, telescope. Which inventions match which dates? Think: Would the compact disc player have been invented before the compact disc?

Extend It

Paper was invented in the year 105. How could you change the timeline in order to show the date of that invention?

Teacher Notes

Extend: Invention Timeline

Objective Make a timeline.

Using the Extend (Activities to use after Lesson 3)
In this activity, students use a timeline to place dates of inventions in order based on year. Critical thinking questions prompt students to decide how to place more dates on their timelines and match up dates with inventions. The Extend It causes students to think about the scale and intervals on their timelines.

Math Journal You may wish to have students use their *Math Journals* to answer the Extend It question.

Going Beyond Have students draw new timelines on a larger scale. Ask them to insert historical or biographical dates and events based on their interests. For example, they might include dates and events involving sports, science, art, literature, technology, politics, etc.

Solutions

See completed timeline below for solutions to Exercises 1, 2, and 3.

Extend It *Answers may vary.*
Sample: You could extend the timeline all the way to the left to the year 100. Be sure to include intervals for all of the years leading up to the year 1500.

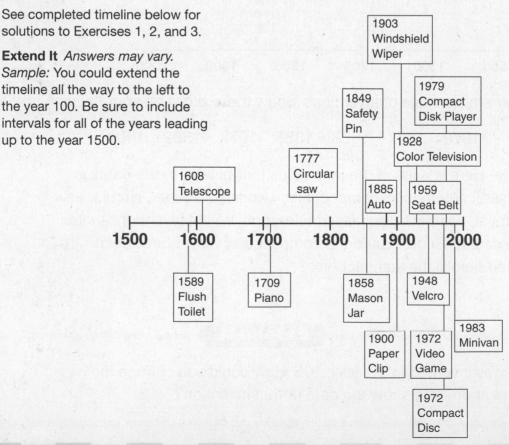

Round Time to Estimate

A CD will be 45 minutes long. The band has chosen 10 tracks it would like to include. Each track and its length in minutes and seconds is listed in this chart. Will all the tracks fit on the CD?

The band members want to estimate the total time of the 10 tracks. First they round each time to the nearest minute.

Look at Track A. *About* how long is it? Think: 6:35 is between 6 minutes and 7 minutes. It is closer to 7 minutes. So, it is *about* 7 minutes long. Remember, there are 60 seconds in a minute.

Round the time of each track to the nearest minute and write the rounded times in the chart.

Track	Time Length (minutes and seconds)	
A	6:35	7 min
B	5:10	_____ min
C	3:02	_____ min
D	4:57	_____ min
E	8:20	_____ min
F	6:29	_____ min
G	7:08	_____ min
H	5:22	_____ min
I	3:59	_____ min
J	5:45	_____ min

The band adds the rounded times to estimate. What is the estimate?

_____ Will all of the tracks fit? _____

1. Round each track time to the nearest 30 seconds.

   About how long are the tracks combined? _____

2. **Predict** Using the track times rounded to the nearest 30 seconds, estimate which tracks might fit on the 45-minute CD.

   _____

Connect It

In what everyday situations might you want to round in order

to make estimates involving time? _____

_____

Teacher Notes

Connect: Round Time to Estimate

Objective Round time given in minutes and seconds to the nearest minute; extend to include rounding to the nearest 30 seconds.

Using the Connect (Activities to use after Lesson 5)
In this activity, students make estimates by rounding amounts of time given in minutes and seconds. They round to the nearest minute, but then see that rounding to the nearest 30 seconds can help them make better estimates. The Connect It helps students relate this skill to everyday activities.

Math Journal You may wish to have students use their *Math Journals* to answer the Connect It question.

Going Beyond Ask students how rounding to the nearest 15 seconds would affect their estimates. They should realize that their estimates would be even more accurate.

Solutions

B: 5 min; C: 3 min; D: 5 min; E: 8 min;
F: 6 min; G: 7 min; H: 5 min; I: 4 min;
J: 6 min
Estimate: 56 min
The tracks will not all fit.

1. A: 6 min 30 sec; B: 5 min;
   C: 3 min; D: 5 min; E: 8 min 30 sec;
   F: 6 min 30 sec; G: 7 min;
   H: 5 min 30 sec; I: 4 min; J: 6 min;
   Total: 57 min

2. *Answers may vary. Sample:* 45 min—
   Tracks A, B, C, E, F, H, I, J

Connect It *Answers may vary. Sample:* When planning a field day, coaches might estimate the total time allotted for various activities being scheduled one after the other to determine if there is enough time for all of them. A chef might estimate total cooking time for various meal components being cooked one after the other to determine if the meal will be ready on time.

Say It With Shapes

You can use symbols in place of numbers to show how math works. In these examples, the symbols are shapes. The square stands for a number, and the triangle stands for a different number. What property of addition does this addition sentence show?

$\triangle + \square = \square + \triangle$ _____

Now let's say $\bigcirc + \square = \triangle$ is true. If so, what property of addition does the addition sentence below show?

$\triangle + \diamondsuit = \triangle$ _____

Use the addition sentences above. Apply what you know about the properties of addition and about the rules of subtraction to complete each exercise.

1. $\bigcirc + \square =$ _____ $+ \bigcirc$

2. $\bigcirc + \square =$ _____

3. $(\bigcirc + \square) + \bigcirc = \bigcirc + ($ _____ $+ \bigcirc)$

4. $\square -$ _____ $= \diamondsuit$

5. $\bigcirc + (\square + \bigcirc) = \bigcirc +$ _____

6. $(\bigcirc + \square) + \bigcirc =$ _____ $+ \bigcirc$

7. **Analyze** Assign values to the symbols in this addition sentence. What do you notice about your choices?

$\square + \diamondsuit = \square$

_____

_____

Explore It

Instead of shapes, use letters and numbers to write addition sentences that show properties of addition. Do the same to show subtraction rules.

Teacher Notes

Explore: Say It With Shapes

Objective Use properties of addition and rules of subtraction.

Using the Explore (Activities to use after Lesson 1)

In this activity, students apply what they know about the properties of addition and rules of subtraction to complete math sentences that use symbols in place of the numbers. In this activity, the symbols are shapes. The critical thinking question tests students' understanding of the Zero Property of Addition. The Explore It introduces students to variables in number sentences.

Math Journal You may wish to have students use their *Math Journals* for the Explore It activity.

Going Beyond Have students use just variables to illustrate the properties and rules.

Solutions

Commutative Property
Zero Property

1. square

2. triangle

3. square

4. square

5. triangle

6. triangle

7. The square can be any number, but the diamond must be zero.

Explore It *Answers may vary. Sample:*
Associative Property of Addition:
$a + (2 + 1) = (a + 2) + 1$

Subtraction rules:
$a - 0 = a$
$a - a = 0$

Add Like the Romans

You have written Roman numerals. Now you will learn to add them.

Here are some Roman numerals with their equivalent Arabic numerals.

I = 1	C = 100	Remember these shortcuts:
V = 5	D = 500	III = 1 + 1 + 1 = 3 XL = 50 − 10 = 40
X = 10	M = 1,000	IV = 5 − 1 = 4 CD = 500 − 100 = 400
L = 50		VI = 5 + 1 = 6 CM = 1,000 − 100 = 900
		IX = 10 − 1 = 9 MC = 1,000 + 100 = 1,100

**Use the shortcuts and what you know about place value
to add. Then find the sum using Arabic numerals.**

1. DXXXII + DCVIII = _____

_____ + _____ = _____

2. MDCXX + MDCCCL = _____

_____ + _____ = _____

3. CCCLVI + MCXXV = _____

_____ + _____ = _____

4. MCCCXXXVI + MMDCIII = _____

_____ + _____ = _____

5. Analyze If you wanted to add the Roman numerals IV and IX,
would you use the numerals written with or without the shortcut?

Why or why not? _____

_____

Extend It

We use the digits 0–9 to write all the numbers in our number
system. Why do you think the Romans used so many letters to
write greater numbers?

Teacher Notes

Extend: Add Like the Romans

Objective Add Roman numerals.

Using the Extend (Activities to use after Lesson 3)

In this activity, students are introduced to one way to add using Roman numerals. Remind students that Arabic numerals are our standard numerals. The critical thinking question asks students to analyze why it is difficult to use addends that are written using shortcuts. For the Extend It, students examine the importance of place value.

Math Journal You may wish to have students use their *Math Journals* to answer the Extend It activity.

Going Beyond Introduce students to the Roman's use of the bar over a symbol. Explain that the bar means they multiply the value of the symbol by 1,000. For example, $\overline{X} = 10,000$.

Solutions

1. MCXL (532 + 608 = 1,140)

2. MMMCDLXX
   (1,620 + 1,850 = 3,470)

3. MCDLXXXI
   (356 + 1,125 = 1,481)

4. MMMCMXXXIX
   (1,336 + 2,603 = 3,939)

5. *Answers may vary. Sample:* I would write the numerals without the shortcut. For example, for IX I write VIIII, and for IV I write IIII. This makes it easier to add the ones.

Extend It *Answers may vary. Sample:* The Romans do not use 0 or place value. Their number system was based on adding and subtracting numbers. That's why they needed to use so many letters for greater numbers.

Clock Arithmetic

Have you ever heard of clock arithmetic?

Here is a 12-hour clock. Use it to add 5 + 9. Start at 5. Move 9 hours ahead, or clockwise.

You end up at _____.

5 + 9 = _____

Now try a 5-hour clock. Using this clock, find 4 + 3.

4 + 3 = _____

Use the clocks to add.

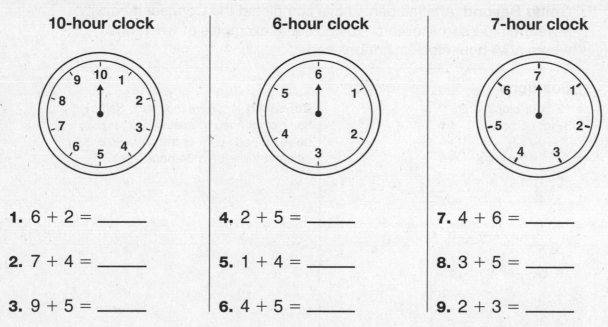

10-hour clock	6-hour clock	7-hour clock

1. 6 + 2 = _____

2. 7 + 4 = _____

3. 9 + 5 = _____

4. 2 + 5 = _____

5. 1 + 4 = _____

6. 4 + 5 = _____

7. 4 + 6 = _____

8. 3 + 5 = _____

9. 2 + 3 = _____

10. Hypothesize Describe how you would use clock arithmetic to subtract.

Connect It

Use a 24-hour clock to write a schedule that shows how you spend the hours in a particular day of the week. Do you need to specify A.M. or P.M. on your schedule?

Teacher Notes

Connect: Clock Arithmetic

Objective Use clock arithmetic to add.

Using the Connect (Activities to use after Lesson 5)
In this activity, students add using clock arithmetic. The critical thinking question has students apply what they have learned about using this method for addition to another operation—in this case, subtraction. The Connect It asks students to use a 24-hour clock to show a schedule of how they spent their time in a day.

Math Journal You may wish to have students use their *Math Journals* for the Connect It activity.

Going Beyond After students have completed the Connect It activity, have them do some research to find some examples of when and where a 24-hour clock might be used.

Solutions

12-hour clock: 2; 2
5-hour clock: 2

1. 8
2. 1
3. 4
4. 1
5. 5
6. 3
7. 3
8. 1
9. 5
10. I would move back, or counterclockwise.

Connect It *Answers may vary. Sample:* You do not need to specify A.M. or P.M. because each hour of the day has a different value on a 24-hour clock.

Commutative Property and Division

Usually you cannot change the order of the numbers in division and get the same quotient. But sometimes you can. Look at the division sentences.

$28 \div 4 \div 1 = ?$ $28 \div 1 \div 4 = ?$

> If a division sentence has 3 numbers, you always divide left to right.

Step 1: Divide the leftmost numbers.

$28 \div 4 \div 1 = ?$ $28 \div 1 \div 4 = ?$
$\quad 7 \div 1 = ?$ $\quad\quad 28 \div 4 = ?$

Step 2: Divide the other terms.

$7 \div 1 = \mathbf{7}$ $28 \div 4 = \mathbf{7}$

Step 3: Look at the quotients.

$7 = 7$

The quotients are equal.

---

1. Describe Explain how the two division sentences above are similar.

_____

Solve if possible.

2. $32 \div 8 \div 2$ $32 \div 2 \div 8$ | **3.** $72 \div 9 \div 8$ $72 \div 8 \div 9$ | **4.** $42 \div 0 \div 6$ $42 \div 6 \div 0$

5. Analyze Were there any exercises you could not solve? If so, explain why you could not solve them.

_____

Explore It

Write division sentences where changing the order of numbers does not give the same quotient. Explain why the Commutative Property works for multiplication and not division.

Teacher Notes

Explore: Commutative Property and Division

Objective Explore how the commutative property relates to division.

Using the Explore (Activities to use after Lesson 1)
Students should gain a deeper understanding of the Commutative Property upon completion of this activity. The activity shows instances in which the Commutative Property works for division. The critical thinking question prompts students to notice the similarities between the division sentences, as well as tie in other rules of division. The Explore It is an opportunity for students to point out inconsistencies with the Commutative Property and division. The Explore It also gives students a better understanding of the Commutative Property and multiplication.

Math Journal You may wish to have students use their *Math Journals* to answer the Explore It question.

Going Beyond Have students write their own division sentences in which the quotients are equal. Make sure their division sentences are made up of three numbers and that the first number in each remains in the same position.

Solutions

1. *Answers may vary. Sample:*
   Both sentences have the same 3 numbers. The number 28 is the first number in each sentence.

2. $32 \div 8 \div 2 = 2$
   $32 \div 2 \div 8 = 2$

3. $72 \div 9 \div 8 = 1$
   $72 \div 8 \div 9 = 1$

4. $42 \div 0 \div 6 =$ no solution
   $42 \div 6 \div 0 =$ no solution

5. *Answers may vary. Sample:*
   You cannot solve the division in Exercise 4 because you cannot divide a number by 0.

Explore It *Answers may vary. Sample:*
$36 \div 6, 6 \div 36$.
36 divided by 6 equals 6. You cannot divide 6 by 36 evenly. This example shows that changing the order of these numbers changes the quotient. The Commutative Property does not work for these numbers. In division, when you change the order of the dividend and divisor, you do not always get the same quotient. The Commutative Property works for multiplication because you can change the order of the factors and still get the same product.

Finding Fact Families

One number can be a part of several fact families.

Bob has 24 cans of corn. He must put an equal amount of cans on a certain number of shelves. Write fact families to show several ways Bob can display the cans.

Way 1: He can display them on 4 shelves with 6 cans on each shelf.

He can display them on 6 shelves with 4 cans on each shelf.

$4 \times 6 = 24$	$24 \div 4 = 6$
$6 \times 4 = 24$	$24 \div 6 = 4$

Way 2: He can display them on 8 shelves with 3 cans on each shelf.

He can display them on 3 shelves with 8 cans on each shelf.

$8 \times 3 = 24$	$24 \div 8 = 3$
$3 \times 8 = 24$	$24 \div 3 = 8$

1. Identify Write two more fact families to show how Bob can display the cans.

_____

Write at least two fact families for each number.

2. 48

_____

_____

_____

_____

3. 72

_____

_____

_____

_____

Extend It

Choose a number for which you can make multiple fact families. Write two fact families for that number. Then write a real life situation where you would use these fact families.

Teacher Notes

Extend: Finding Fact Families

Objective Find fact families for given numbers.

Using the Extend (Activities to use after Lesson 3)
This activity teaches children about fact families and indirectly introduces multiples. Students identify fact families for given numbers. In the process, they find factors of that number. In the Extend It students find a fact family on their own and connect it to a real world scenario.

Math Journal You may wish to have students use their *Math Journals* for the Extend It.

Going Beyond Have students find fact families for all the numbers 1 through 9. Students may notice that each odd number and the number 2 have only one fact family and that the numbers 4, 6, 8, and 10 each have exactly two fact families.

Solutions

1. $12 \times 2 = 24$ $24 \div 12 = 2$
   $2 \times 12 = 24$ $24 \div 2 = 12$

   $24 \times 1 = 24$ $24 \div 24 = 1$
   $1 \times 24 = 24$ $24 \div 1 = 24$

2. *Answers may vary. Sample:*
   $8 \times 6 = 48$ $48 \div 8 = 6$
   $6 \times 8 = 48$ $48 \div 6 = 8$

   $12 \times 4 = 48$ $48 \div 4 = 12$
   $4 \times 12 = 48$ $48 \div 12 = 4$

3. *Answers may vary. Sample:*
   $9 \times 8 = 72$ $72 \div 9 = 8$
   $8 \times 9 = 72$ $72 \div 8 = 9$

   $12 \times 6 = 72$ $72 \div 12 = 6$
   $6 \times 12 = 72$ $72 \div 6 = 12$

Extend It *Answers may vary. Sample:*
The number chosen is 36.

$9 \times 4 = 36$ $36 \div 9 = 4$
$4 \times 9 = 36$ $36 \div 4 = 9$

$12 \times 3 = 36$ $36 \div 12 = 3$
$3 \times 12 = 36$ $36 \div 3 = 12$

Alison does not know how to display her 36 toys. She wants an equal number of toys on each of a certain number of shelves. Write fact families to show several ways she can display the toys.

Name _____ Date _____

Number Names

You can give a number different "names" by writing an
expression. Look at the different ways you can write 16.

$$4 \times 4 \qquad 2 \times 2 \times 4 \qquad 32 \div 4 \times 2$$

Here are names for 16 that use the numbers 2, 4, and 8.

Way 1: $8 \times 4 \div 2$	**Way 2:** $4 \div 2 \times 8$
$8 \times 4 = \mathbf{32}$	$4 \div 2 = \mathbf{2}$
$\mathbf{32} \div 2 = 16$	$\mathbf{2} \times 8 = 16$

Solve the problems below using the following rules.

- You can use only multiplication and division symbols.
- You can arrange the numbers in any order.
- You must use all the numbers given exactly once.

1. Find another name for 25 using the numbers 4, 4, 5, and 5. _____

2. Find another name for 28 using the numbers 2, 2, 9, and 63. _____

3. Find another name for 36 using the numbers 2, 3, and 6. _____

4. Find another name for 72 using the numbers 2, 6, 6, and 36. _____

5. Find another name for 100 using the numbers 2, 2, 5, and 5. _____

Connect It

Does changing the order of numbers in a division or multiplication
problem affect the answer? Explain whether changing the order
of the numbers can change your answer.

Teacher Notes

Connect: Number Names

Objective Write numbers different ways using multiplication and division expressions.
Materials calculator

Using the Connect (Activities to use after Lesson 5)
Students are given a number and write the number different ways using multiplication and division expressions and other numbers they are also given. In this activity, students use multiplication and division together to create expressions. The Connect It asks students to examine how the Commutative Property is connected to multiplication and/or division.

Math Journal You may wish to have students use their *Math Journals* to answer the Connect It question.

Going Beyond Have students create their own problems similar to the ones in the activity. Students should choose a two- or three-digit number and write expressions that use at least 3 numbers.

Solutions

Answers may vary. Sample:

1. $5 \times 4 \times 5 \div 4$

2. $63 \div 9 \times 2 \times 2$

3. $2 \times 3 \times 6$

4. $36 \div 6 \times 6 \times 2$

5. $5 \times 5 \times 2 \times 2$

Connect It When you change the order of the numbers in a division problem, the quotient changes. When you change the order of the numbers in a multiplication problem, the product does not change. This is because of the Commutative Property. Multiplication is commutative. Division is not commutative.

What's Missing?

Look at the number sentence below.
The operations are missing.

$$18 \blacksquare 2 \blacksquare 9 = 180$$

You can use operations and parentheses to make
the sentence true. $(18 + 2) \times 9 = 180$

You can use the symbols $+$, $-$, $\times$, and $\div$. You may also need to use parentheses,
like in the example above. Note: There may be more than one way to make some
number sentences true. Remember the order of operations!

1. $15 \blacksquare 6 \blacksquare 3 = 3$ _____

2. $8 \blacksquare 3 \blacksquare 4 = 20$ _____

3. $9 \blacksquare 21 \blacksquare 3 = 16$ _____

4. $5 \blacksquare 5 \blacksquare 10 \blacksquare 5 \blacksquare = 20$ _____

5. $7 \blacksquare 1 \blacksquare 6 = 1$ _____

6. $9 \blacksquare 2 \blacksquare 3 = 33$ _____

7. $5 \blacksquare 2 \blacksquare 5 \blacksquare = 15$ _____

8. $12 \blacksquare 4 \blacksquare 2 \blacksquare 1 = 24$ _____

9. $8 \blacksquare 4 \blacksquare 2 \blacksquare 1 = 15$ _____

10. $2 \blacksquare 6 \blacksquare 7 \blacksquare 4 \blacksquare 2 = 12$ _____

11. Create Following the order of operations, you find that the expressions
$4 \times (2 + 1)$ and $(5 \times 3) - 3$ are of equal value. Write two expressions that
are *not* of equal value. Then use $>$ or $<$ to compare them.

_____

Explore It

Compare how you use parentheses in math with how you use
them in writing, such as: Mr. Dixon (our math teacher) is giving
a test today. How are they the same? How are they different?

Teacher Notes

Explore: What's Missing?

Objective Use order of operations to complete number sentences.

Using the Explore (Activities to use after Lesson 1)
In this activity, students are given number sentences whose operation signs, sometimes including parentheses, are missing. They use what they know about order of operations to make the number sentences true. The critical thinking question requires students to generate number sentences that are not true and compare them using $>$ or $<$. The Explore It asks students to compare how parentheses are used in math to how they are used in writing.

Math Journal You may wish to have students use their *Math Journals* to answer the Explore It question.

Going Beyond For the Explore It, have students look up the meaning and derivation of parentheses in a dictionary. Then have them find or make up some sentences in which they are used in writing, and list them alongside some examples in which they are used in math, before they make the comparison.

Solutions

Answers may vary. Sample answers given below.

1. $(15 - 6) \div 3 = 3$
2. $8 + (3 \times 4) = 20$
3. $9 + (21 \div 3) = 16$
4. $(5 + 5) \times 10 \div 5 = 20$
5. $7 - (1 \times 6) = 1$
6. $(9 + 2) \times 3 = 33$
7. $5 \times 2 + 5 = 15$
8. $12 + 4 \times (2 + 1) = 24$
9. $8 \times 4 \div 2 - 1 = 15$
10. $(2 + 6) \times (7 - 4) \div 2 = 12$
11. *Answers may vary. Sample:*
    $3 + 5 \times 2 < (3 + 5) \times 2$

Explore It Some students may notice that in both math and writing, parentheses indicate and set apart a piece of information. In writing, the parentheses and the information within do not change the meaning of the sentence; in math they do.

What's the Story?

Look at this expression: $2 \times (n + 2)$.

Here is a story to go with it: Aisha spent 2 hours more than Dan on an art project. Greg spent twice as long as Aisha on the art project.

If n represents the number of hours Dan spent on the art project, then $n + 2$ represents the number of hours Aisha spent on the art project. The expression $2 \times (n + 2)$ represents how long Greg spent on the project.

Make up some stories of your own for the expressions below. Then write what the expression represents. Maybe you would like to write a story related to the sports or games you play. You could write about hobbies, family, school, money, or food.

1. $80 \times (t - 3)$ _____

_____

2. $l \times (l - 3)$ _____

_____

3. $(s + 5) \div 9$ _____

_____

4. $4b + 3$ _____

_____

5. Create Let $a = 3$. Write two different expressions that have the same value, for example $a + 2$ and $15 \div a$.

Extend It

Choose a value for each of the variables in the expressions used in Exercises 1 through 4 above. Evaluate the expressions.

Teacher Notes

Extend: What's the Story?

Objective Provide story problems for expressions.

Using the Extend (Activities to use after Lesson 3)
In this chapter, students have been writing expressions with variables in order to describe various situations presented to them. In this activity, students are given the expressions and are asked to create stories to go with them. The critical thinking question has students write two expressions that are different yet have the same value. The Extend It asks students to evaluate the expressions they used for their stories.

Math Journal You may wish to have students use their *Math Journals* for the Extend It activity.

Going Beyond Have students write 4 expressions, each using a different operation, that each have the same value.

Solutions

1. *Answers may vary. Sample:* Theater tickets were discounted $3. 80 people bought tickets. The expression tells how much money the theater collected for tickets.

2. *Answers may vary. Sample:* The width of a garden is 3 feet less than its length. The expression tells the area of the garden.

3. *Answers may vary. Sample:* There are 5 more students in the third grade than in the fourth grade. A teacher gathered all of the third grade students together and made 9 lines with the same number of students in each. The expression tells the number of students in each line.

4. *Answers may vary. Sample:* A librarian read the same number of books to students in an after-school group each week for 4 weeks. The next week she read 3 more books. The expression tells the number of books the librarian read in all.

5. *Answers may vary. Sample:* $a - 1$ and $6 \div a$

Extend It *Answers may vary. Sample:* Be sure students choose reasonable values. For the sample answer to Exercise 1 given above, a good choice might be $80 \times (7 - 3)$, $7 being a realistic price for a ticket. $80 \times (7 - 3) = 320$. The theater collected $320.

Inequality Challenge

Here's a way to solve for *n* when you have an inequality.

Solve $n + 3 > 5$.
Choose from the numbers 0, 1, 2, 3, 4, and 5 for *n*.

Start trying the numbers on the list. Start with 0.

Try 0.

$0 + 3 > 5$

$3 > 5$

Is the inequality true?
No, it isn't. So try the next
number on the list, 1.

Try 1.

$\rule{1cm}{0.4pt} + 3 > 5$

$\rule{1cm}{0.4pt} > 5$

Is the inequality true? _____

Keep trying all of the numbers on the list until you find the
number or numbers that make the inequality true.

Write the solution here: $n = $ _____

**Now try these. Find *n*. This time choose from the numbers
0, 1, 2, 3, 4, 5, 6, 7, 8, 9, and 10.**

1. $n + 2 < 6$

$n = $ _____

2. $n \div 4 > 1$

$n = $ _____

3. $5n < 10$

$n = $ _____

4. $n - 1 < 9$

$n = $ _____

5. $4n > 8$

$n = $ _____

6. $n \div 1 < 10$

$n = $ _____

7. Predict What would the solution to $n + 3 > 5$ be if you could choose

from all whole numbers, instead of just 0, 1, 2, 3, 4, and 5? _____

Connect It

Try making up and solving some inequalities using $\neq$ for $>$ and $<$.
Choose from 0, 1, 2, 3, 4, 5, 6, 7, 8, 9, and 10 for *n*.

Teacher Notes

Connect: Inequality Challenge

Objective Solve inequalities, given a replacement set.

Using the Connect (Activities to use after Lesson 5)
In this activity, students solve inequalities involving $>$ and $<$, given a replacement set. The critical thinking question asks students to predict what would happen if the replacement set were all of the whole numbers. The Connect It has students write and solve inequalities involving $\neq$.

Math Journal You may wish to have students use their *Math Journals* for the Connect It activity.

Going Beyond For the Connect It, first have students replace the $>$ and $<$ signs with $\neq$ in the inequalities in the exercises and solve. After that practice, they can then make up their own inequalities using $\neq$ and solve those.

Solutions

1; 4; no; 3, 4, 5

1. 0, 1, 2, 3

2. 5, 6, 7, 8, 9, 10

3. 0, 1

4. 0, 1, 2, 3, 4, 5, 6, 7, 8, 9

5. 3, 4, 5, 6, 7, 8, 9, 10

6. 0, 1, 2, 3, 4, 5, 6, 7, 8, 9

7. *Answers may vary. Sample:* The solutions are all whole numbers greater than or equal to 3.

Connect It *Answers may vary. Sample:* $n + 3 \neq 5$; $n = 0, 1, 3, 4, 5, 6, 7, 8, 9, 10$.

Factor Fill-In

You can use basic facts and patterns of zeros to
help you multiply. Here's your chance to prove it.
One factor is missing below. Fill it in fast!

$2 \times 900 = 3 \times$ _____

To solve, first find the product on the left. Use basic
facts and patterns of zeros.
Think: $2 \times 9 = 18$, $2 \times 90 = 180$,
and $2 \times 900 = 1,800$.

The equal sign tells you that the product on the right
has to be equal to the product on the left. In this
case the product is 1,800.
Think: $3 \times ? = 18$. Then, $3 \times 6 = 18$,
$3 \times 60 = 180$, and $3 \times 600 = 1,800$.

So, $2 \times 900 = 3 \times 600$.

Find the missing factor.

1. $3 \times 800 =$ _____ $\times 600$

2. $2 \times 3,000 = 6 \times$ _____

3. $4 \times$ _____ $= 2 \times 8,000$

4. _____ $\times 100 = 4 \times 200$

5. $8 \times 70,000 = 7 \times$ _____

6. $9 \times$ _____ $= 6 \times 6,000$

7. _____ $\times 30 = 6 \times 20$

8. $6 \times 50,000 = 3 \times$ _____

9. **Analyze** Try $4 \times 600 = 80 \times$ _____. Hint: In this example,
   the number of zeros in the product is the same as the number
   of zeros in the factors.

Explore It

Construct three function tables for the rule $5a = b$. In the first
table, input some multiples of 10. In the second table, input some
multiples of 100. In the third table, input some multiples of 1,000.

Teacher Notes

Explore: Factor Fill-In

Objective Find missing factors when multiplying with multiples of 10, 100, and 1,000.

Using the Explore (Activities to use after Lesson 1)
In this activity, students find missing factors in number sentences. They use basic facts and patterns of zeros to find the missing factors. The critical thinking question uses patterns of zeros to introduce students to two-digit multiplication. The Explore It asks students to construct function tables for a given rule and input multiples of 10, 100, and 1,000.

Math Journal You may wish to have students use their *Math Journals* for the Explore It activity.

Going Beyond For the Explore It, have students choose at least 3 inputs. They can use any multiples of 10, 100, and 1,000. Discuss any "extra" zeros they may notice in the patterns of zeros in their tables.

Solutions

1. 4

2. 1,000

3. 4,000

4. 8

5. 80,000

6. 4,000

7. 4

8. 100,000

9. 30

Explore It *Answers may vary. Sample:* For inputs 10, 20, 30, the outputs are 50, 100, 150 respectively. For inputs 100, 200, 300, the outputs are 500, 1,000, 1,500 respectively. For inputs 1,000, 2,000, 3,000, the outputs are 5,000, 10,000, 15,000 respectively.

Lattice Multiplication

Here's a way to multiply without using base-ten blocks. It's called lattice multiplication. You do all your work in a grid that looks like the crossed pieces of a lattice. Use it to multiply 4 × 85.

First, make your lattice. The factor 4 has one digit. The factor 85 has two digits. So, make your lattice one-by-two. Label the sides with the factors, as shown.

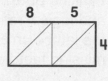

Next, draw a diagonal in each square.

Now you are ready to start multiplying. Begin at the right: 4 × 5 = 20. Write 20 in the right-hand square. Write 2 above the diagonal. Write 0 below the diagonal. Then multiply 4 × 8 = 32. Write 32 in the next square.

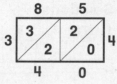

The next step is to add the numbers in the diagonals and write the sums around the lattice.

Finally, read the product. Start at the left and read down and across the bottom: 340. So, 4 × 85 = 340.

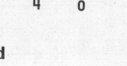

Use lattice multiplication to find each product. You'll need a separate sheet of paper to make your lattices.

1. 5 × 35 = _____

2. 9 × 64 = _____

3. 7 × 53 = _____

4. 2 × 99 = _____

5. 6 × 47 = _____

6. 3 × 75 = _____

7. Explain You filled in the squares of your lattices with two-digit numbers. What should you do if you have a one-digit number to write in a square of a lattice? Try 2 × 36.

Extend It

On a separate sheet of paper, make and complete three examples of lattice multiplication.

Teacher Notes

Extend: Lattice Multiplication

Objective Use lattice multiplication to multiply.

Using the Extend (Activities to use after Lesson 3)
In this activity, students are introduced to lattice multiplication and use it to multiply two-digit numbers by one-digit numbers. The critical thinking question has students use what they know about place value and logical reasoning to explain how to position a one-digit number in the lattice. In Extend It, students create their own lattices to find a missing factor.

Math Journal You may wish to have students use their *Math Journals* for the Extend It activity.

Going Beyond Have students try lattice multiplication to multiply greater numbers.

Solutions

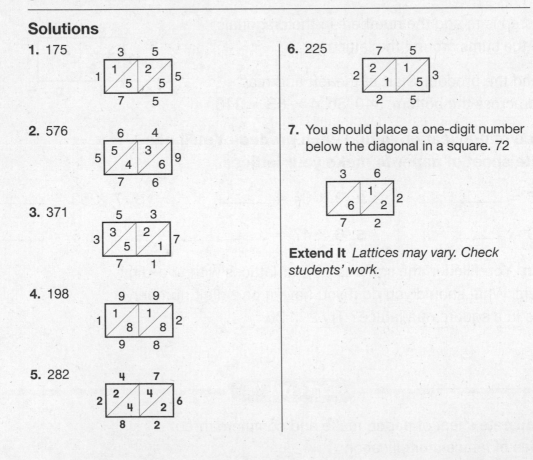

1. 175

2. 576

3. 371

4. 198

5. 282

6. 225

7. You should place a one-digit number below the diagonal in a square. 72

Extend It *Lattices may vary. Check students' work.*

Fair Exchange

Ann e-mailed Keiko in Japan to say that she bought a book for $9.
Keiko e-mailed back that she bought the same book for 1,044 yen.
The girls wondered why the two book prices were so different. They did
some research. They looked up the foreign exchange rate and found that,
on the day they made their purchases, $1 was worth about 116 yen. So,
it cost about 116 times as many yen as dollars to buy the same book.
The girls multiplied to compare the prices of the book.

$$9 \times 116 = 1,044$$

cost of book   number of yen   cost of book
in dollars   for each dollar   in yen

They realized the price of the books was
the same!

Ann looked up the exchange rates for other
countries. Here's her list of about what $1
was worth on that same day in those countries
and the names of their currencies.

Country	Name of currency	Exchange rate per $1
Japan	yen	116
Zambia	kwacha	4,696
Iceland	kronur	73
Romania	lei	32,553
Egypt	pounds	6

Use the list to find the cost of the items.

1. a $125 coat cost in pounds _____

2. a $9 video game cost in kronur _____

3. a $3 bowl of soup, a $4 sandwich, and a $2 glass of juice cost in lei _____

   _____

4. three $4 notebooks cost in kwacha. _____

5. **Compare and Contrast** Keiko noticed that a year ago $1 was
   worth 128 yen. If she had exchanged yen for dollars, would she
   have received more or fewer dollars last year than this year? _____

Connect It

Every day for a week, look in a newspaper or on the Internet to
find the foreign currency exchange rates for the countries listed above
and for other countries of your choice. Keep a record. What do you notice?

Teacher Notes

Connect: Fair Exchange

Objective Find prices of items using different currencies.

Using the Connect (Activities to use after Lesson 5)

In this activity, students find what items priced in dollars would cost in foreign currencies. The critical thinking question has them determine what happens to one currency when the exchange rate changes. The Connect It has students look up and keep track of the exchange rate over a period of time.

Math Journal You may wish to have students use their *Math Journals* to answer the Connect It question.

Going Beyond Ask students to find out what happens to the value of their money if they travel when the dollar is strong versus when the dollar is weak. They should discover that when the dollar is strong, it will take fewer dollars to buy an item priced in a foreign currency; when the dollar is weak, it will take more dollars.

Solutions

1. 750 pounds

2. 657 kronur

3. 97,659 (soup) + 130,212 (sandwich) + 65,106 (juice) = 292,977 lei

4. 3 × 18,784 = 56,352 kwacha

5. fewer dollars

Connect It *Answers may vary.* Students should notice that the exchange rates vary. They either went up or down.

Multiplication Puzzle

You can use basic facts and patterns of zeros to solve puzzles.
In the puzzles below, each number is the product of two pairs
of factors. In each pair of factors, at least one factor is a multiple
of 10, 100, or 1,000.

Solve the puzzle.

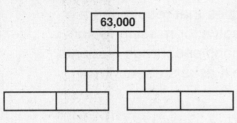

Be sure you use
basic facts to find
each pair of factors.

1. What did you notice about the number of zeros in each product?

_____

Now solve this puzzle.

2. What is different about
the number of zeros in the
product in this puzzle?

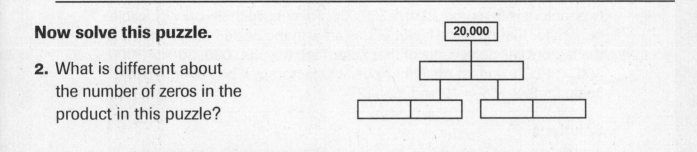

_____

3. Analyze Is there a different way you could have solved the

puzzle in Exercise 2? Explain. _____

Solve the puzzles.

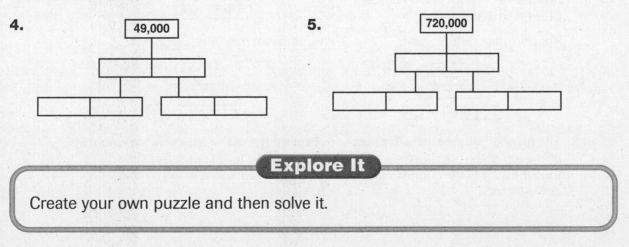

4. 49,000

5. 720,000

Explore It

Create your own puzzle and then solve it.

Teacher Notes

Explore: Multiplication Puzzle

Objective Use basic facts and patterns of zero to identify missing factors.

Using the Explore (Activities to use after Lesson 1)

Students used basic facts and patterns of zero to multiply factors of ten. In this activity, students complete puzzles that require them to use the same mental math techniques to solve for missing factors when given a product. Critical thinking questions encourage students to look beyond a single solution. The Explore It asks students to create a puzzle of their own.

Math Journal You may wish to have students use their *Math Journals* to answer the Explore It activity.

Going Beyond Ask students to find how many zeros would be in two factors with a product of 1,200,000. Then, have them offer possible factors for that product. If students start with the basic fact $3 \times 4 = 12$, the factors will be variants of that basic fact: $3 \times 400,000$; $30 \times 40,000$; $300 \times 4,000$; and so on. Other possible factors will be variants of the basic facts $2 \times 6 = 12$ and $1 \times 12 = 12$.

Solutions

Answers may vary. Sample:

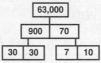

1. The number of zeros in the product is equal to the sum of the number of zeros in the factors.

   Answers may vary. Sample:

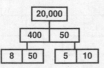

2. The number of zeros in the product at the top of the puzzle is one greater than the sum of the number of zeros in the factors.

3. *Answers may vary. Sample:* Yes. I could have used different factors to make the same products.

4. *Answers may vary. Sample:*

5. *Answers may vary. Sample:*

Explore It *Puzzles may vary, but should be based on using basic facts and patterns of zero to find the missing numbers.*

Mental-Math Multiplication

You can use this math trick to multiply two-digit numbers
mentally. Break apart one factor and multiply to find each
product. Then add.

Here is how you can use mental multiplication to find 23×35.

Remember
The Distributive
Property lets you break
factors apart.

First, break apart the first factor so that one part
is a multiple of 10.

$23 \times 35 = (20 \times 35) + (\text{\_\_\_\_} \times 35)$

Then multiply to find each product.   Finally, add the products.

$20 \times 35 = \text{\_\_\_\_}$ $\text{\_\_\_\_} + \text{\_\_\_\_} = 805$

$\text{\_\_\_\_} \times 35 = \text{\_\_\_\_}$ $23 \times 35 = 805$

1. Suppose the order of the factors was changed to 35×23.
Would it be easier or harder to multiply mentally? Try it.

_____

2. Analyze Is there a different way you could have found the

product of 23×35? Explain. _____

_____

Multiply mentally.

3. 21×45 **4.** 12×13 **5.** 34×25 **6.** 11×34

Extend It

Make up two multiplication problems with two-digit factors.
Use each of these four digits exactly once: 1 3 2 5. One
problem should be easy to solve mentally, and one should
be more difficult. Solve your problems. Explain why one
is more difficult to solve mentally than the other.

Teacher Notes

Extend: Mental-Math Multiplication

Objective Use the Distributive Property to multiply two-digit numbers.

Using the Extend (Activities to use after Lesson 3)

Students use the Distributive Property to break apart the first factor into a multiple of 10 and a number less than 10. They can then mentally multiply the partial products and add them to find the total product. Mental math "tricks" such as this one are fun for students and help them break apart and analyze products. Critical thinking questions encourage students to look beyond a single solution. The Extend It asks students to create mental math problems of their own.

Math Journal You may wish to have students use their *Math Journals* for the Extend It activity.

Going Beyond Give students real-world multiplication exercises with two-digit factors and have students solve them mentally. For example, they can estimate the number of students in the school if the average class size is 24 students.

Solutions

$23 \times 35 = (20 \times 35) + (3 \times 35)$
$20 \times 35 = 700 \quad 3 \times 35 = 105$
$700 + 105 = 805$

1. *Answers may vary. Sample:* It is harder to multiply 35×23 because when you break apart the first factor you get $(30 \times 23) + (5 \times 23)$ which is not as easy to solve mentally.

2. *Answers may vary.* Students may point out another way to break apart the factors. They might also describe how to use models to multiply or they might use the multiplication algorithm.

3. 21×45
   $(20 \times 45) + (1 \times 45) = 945$

4. 12×13
   $(10 \times 13) + (2 \times 13) = 156$

5. 34×25
   $(30 \times 25) + (4 \times 25) = 850$

6. 11×34
   $(10 \times 34) + (1 \times 34) = 374$

Extend It *Answers may vary. Sample:* An easy problem to solve mentally: $13 \times 25 = 325$. A harder problem to solve mentally: $32 \times 51 = 1,632$. The second problem is more difficult because the factors don't break apart into numbers that are as easy to multiply as 10×25.

Finding Area

Lucille wants to replace the floor in her kitchen, hall, and foyer with ceramic tiles. Each tile is 1 foot square. Here is a diagram of Lucille's kitchen, hall, and foyer.

Remember
Lucille does not need to tile the kitchen island.

KITCHEN

KITCHEN ISLAND

HALL

**KEY:
EACH ☐ IS
1 FT SQUARE**

FOYER

1. How many tiles will Lucille need to tile just the kitchen? Explain.

————————————————————————

————————————————————————

2. How many tiles will Lucille need to tile the kitchen, the hall, and

the foyer? Explain. ————————————————————

3. Tiles are sold by the box. Each box contains 14 tiles. How many boxes should Lucille buy to tile the kitchen, the hall, and the foyer? ——————

How did you find the answer? ——————————————

4. Compare Lucille is choosing between two kinds of tiles. The Sand Tiles cost $28 per box. It will cost $523 to tile the entire area using the White Tiles. Which is less expensive? Explain.

————————————————————————

————————————————————————

Connect It

Suppose the school wants to tile your classroom. Measure its length and width in feet. Find how many tiles you would need. Then find how many boxes of tile at 14 tiles per box you would need to buy.

Teacher Notes

Connect: Finding Area

Objective Multiply two-digit numbers to solve area problems.

Using the Connect (Activities to use after Lesson 5)
In this activity, students use data in a diagram to solve real-world area problems. The problems are constructed so that students can take different approaches to find solutions. The Connect It asks students to measure the classroom, then compute how many tiles it would take to tile the classroom.

Math Journal You may wish to have students use their *Math Journals* to answer the Connect It.

Going Beyond Have students find the current price of ceramic tiles, rounded to the nearest dollar. Have them compute the cost of tiling Lucille's kitchen, hall, and foyer.

Solutions

1. 204 tiles; *Answers may vary. Sample:* Lucille needs tiles to cover the area of the kitchen minus the area of the island. Students can count tiles or multiply to find each area, then subtract: $(18 \times 12) - (3 \times 4) = 204$.

2. *Answers may vary. Sample:* Lucille needs 284 tiles to cover the floor of the kitchen, the hall, and the foyer: $204 + (4 \times 12) + (4 \times 8) = 284$.

3. 21 boxes; *Answers may vary.* Students can find the answer by writing a number sentence and using the guess, test, and revise strategy to find the missing factor: $14 \times ? = 284$. They will find that $14 \times 20 = 280$ and $14 \times 21 = 294$. So, Lucille needs 20 boxes plus 4 more tiles. Since Lucille must buy the tiles in boxes of 14 each, she must buy 21 boxes.

4. The White Tiles; The Sand Tiles are $28 per box, so 21 boxes will cost $588. So, the White Tiles, which cost $523, are less expensive.

Connect It *Answers may vary based on the size of the classroom.* You may need to tell students how to find area: multiply the length by the width to find the area in square feet. Students should subtract any areas that do not need to be tiled. Students might also need to talk about rounding if the length and/or the width of the classroom is not a whole number of feet.

Multiplication and Division

You can use the relationship between multiplication
and division to solve division problems.

What is $39 \div 3$?
Use counters to show 39.
Divide 39 into 3 equal groups.

Write a number sentence to show the division. _____ $\div$ _____ = _____

Then, write a related multiplication sentence. _____ $\times$ _____ = 39

1. Look at the dividend, divisor, and quotient in the division
sentence. How are they related to the factors and product

in the multiplication sentence? _____

_____

_____

2. Now use counters to find $39 \div 4$. Write a number sentence

to show the division. _____ $\div$ _____ = _____ R_____

3. Can you write a related multiplication sentence that includes

the remainder? Try it. _____

> **Think**
> You can add
> the remainder
> to the factors to
> get 39.

4. Apply How can you use a multiplication sentence to check

your answer to a division sentence? Give an example. _____

_____

Use counters or multiplication to divide.

5. $25 \div 2 =$ _____ **6.** $60 \div 4 =$ _____ **7.** $75 \div 3 =$ _____ **8.** $32 \div 3 =$ _____

Explore It

Explain how you would find what factor times 4 equals 72.

Teacher Notes

Explore: Multiplication and Division

Objective Relate division and multiplication.

Using the Explore (Activities to use after Lesson 1)

Multiplication and division are inverse operations—one operation undoes the other. In this activity, students explore the relationship between division and multiplication and discover that related division and multiplication sentences can be used to solve one another. Critical thinking questions encourage students to apply what they discover to different situations. The Explore It asks students to use a related division sentence to find a missing factor.

Math Journal You may wish to have students use their *Math Journals* for the Explore It activity.

Going Beyond Have students find at least two ways to solve the division problem $100 \div 4$. For example, they could use the multiplication sentence $25 \times 4 = 100$, or they could show 4 groups of 25 counters each to find that $100 \div 4 = 25$.

Solutions

$39 \div 3 = 13$

$3 \times 13 = 39$

1. *Answers may vary. Sample:* The dividend becomes the product of the multiplication sentence, and the divisor and quotient become the factors.

2. $39 \div 4 = 9$ R3

3. Yes, but you must add the remainder: $(4 \times 9) + 3 = 39$.

4. *Answers may vary. Sample:* Multiply the quotient times the divisor. The result should be the dividend. For example, you can use the multiplication sentence $12 \times 2 = 24$ to check that $24 \div 2 = 12$ is correct.

5. 12 R1

6. 15

7. 25

8. 10 R2

Explore It *Answers may vary. Sample:* First, I will divide 72 into 4 equal groups. Once I know that $72 \div 4 = 18$, I can find that $18 \times 4 = 72$. So, the missing factor is 18.

Short Division

In short division, you do more computation mentally.

Here is how to use short division to find the quotient of 74 divided by 6.

	Think	Write	Example
Step 1:	$6\overline{)7}$ is about 1. 1 times 6 is 6. 7 minus 6 is 1.	Write 1 above the 7. Write a small 1 to the left of the 4 in the dividend.	$\dfrac{1}{6\overline{)7_14}}$
Step 2:	$6\overline{)14}$ is about 2. 2 times 6 is 12. 14 minus 12 is 2.	Write 2 above the 4. The remainder is 2.	$\dfrac{1\ 2}{6\overline{)7_14}}$ R2

Use short division to find each quotient.

1. $5\overline{)5\ 6}$ 2. $8\overline{)9\ 2}$ 3. $3\overline{)4\ 6}$ 4. $2\overline{)7\ 5}$

5. $4\overline{)6\ 8}$ 6. $6\overline{)8\ 7}$ 7. $5\overline{)7\ 7}$ 8. $3\overline{)5\ 3}$

9. How is short division like long division? How is it different?

_____

_____

_____

10. **Analyze** When would you use short division? Why? _____

_____

Extend It

Is short division really quicker? Write two different division problems
with one-digit divisors and three-digit dividends. Time yourself solving
each problem, using the short division method for one problem and
the long division method for the other.

Teacher Notes

Extend: Short Division

Objective Use short division and mental computation to divide.

Using the Extend (Activities to use after Lesson 3)

Students use short division to find quotients for problems with one-digit divisors and two-digit dividends. This method encourages mental computation and saves time for students, which is useful when taking a standardized test that does not allow calculators. Critical thinking questions ask students to compare short and long division. The Extend It asks students to extend the method to a problem with a three-digit dividend.

Math Journal You may wish to have students use their *Math Journals* for the Extend It activity.

Going Beyond Have students use short division to find the quotient of 1,548 ÷ 4. (387) They should see that they can use the same method, and simply extend it to one more place.

Solutions

1. *Answers may vary. Sample:* They are the same because both methods use multiplication, then subtraction, to solve. They are different because with short division you only record the results of each computation as the quotient and remainder, while with long division you record all the computations for each step.

2. *Answers may vary. Sample:* Use short division to get a quick answer when the division is relatively simple, such as a divisor less than 10 and two- or three-digit dividends.

3. 11 R1

4. 11 R4

5. 15 R1

6. 37 R1

7. 17

8. 14 R3

9. 15 R2

10. 17 R2

Extend It *Answers may vary.*

Name _____ Date _____

The Mayan Calendar

The Maya had two calendars. One was a 260-day cycle called the tzolkin. The other was a 365-day cycle called the haab. The haab was divided into months (uinals) of 20 days plus one month of 5 "nameless" days. The nameless days were considered very unlucky.

Complete the chart at right. Then answer the questions below.

The Mayan Calendar (Haab)
1 kin = 1 day
1 uinal = 20 kin = 20 days
1 tun = _____ uinal = 360 days
1 katun = _____ tun = 7,200 days
1 baktun = 20 katun = _____ days

1. How many modern months are in 6 uinal? (Use one month = 30 days.) Show how you got the answer.

   _____

   _____

2. How many modern months are in 1 tun? (Use one month = 30 days.)

   Show how you got the answer. _____

   _____

3. About how many modern years is 1 katun? _____

4. About how many modern years is one baktun? _____

5. The Pyramid of Kulkulkan was built around 1050 by the Maya, who used it as a calendar. The pyramid has 4 stairways. Each stairway has the same number of steps, plus a platform at the top, making a total of 365, the number of days in a year. How many steps does each stairway have? Explain.

   _____

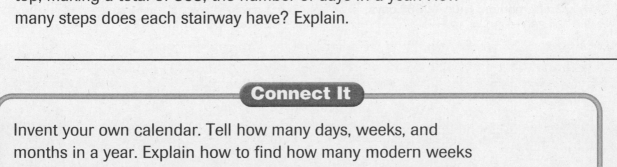

Connect It

Invent your own calendar. Tell how many days, weeks, and months in a year. Explain how to find how many modern weeks equal 1 week in your calendar, and how many modern months equal 1 month in your calendar.

Teacher Notes

Connect: The Mayan Calendar

Objective Solve multi-step word problems using division and multiplication.

Using the Connect (Activities to use after Lesson 5)

In this activity, students learn about the Mayan calendar and convert Mayan days and years to modern days. The problems are constructed so that students can take different approaches to their solutions. The Connect It asks students to invent their own calendars.

Math Journal You may wish to have students use their *Math Journals* to show the calendars they invent for the Connect It activity.

Going Beyond Have students research other calendar systems, such as the Jewish calendar or the Chinese calendar. Ask them to create their own math Connect worksheet using this information.

Solutions

The Mayan Year (Haab)
1 kin = 1 day
1 uinal = 20 kin = 20 days
1 tun = 18 uinal = 360 days
1 katun = 20 tun = 7,200 days
1 baktun = 20 katun = 144,000 days

1. 4 months; 1 uinal = 20 days;
   6 uinals = 6 × 20 = 120 days;
   120 ÷ 30 = 4

2. 12 months; 1 tun = 360 days;
   360 ÷ 30 = 12

3. about 20 years

4. about 400 years

5. Each stairway has 91 steps. I found the answer by subtracting 1 for the platform from 365. Then I divided 364 by 4 to get 91 steps per stairway.

Connect It *Answers may vary. Students' calendars should be based on a 365-day year, and include a logical system of days, weeks, and months.*

Add to Divide

Did you know that sometimes you can use addition to divide? Try it.

Remember
A number is divisible if it can be divided into equal parts and there is no remainder.

Add to find 105 ÷ 7.

First, write 105 as two addends divisible by 7.

105 = _____ + _____

Next, divide each addend by 7.

_____ ÷ 7 = _____

_____ ÷ 7 = _____

Finally, add the quotients.

_____ + _____ = 15

105 ÷ 7 = 15

1. Find as many other ways as you can to break apart 105 to form two addends divisible by 7. _____

_____

2. **Analyze** Do you think you found all the pairs of addends divisible by 7 that have the sum of 105? Explain. _____

_____

Use addition to divide.

3. 654 ÷ 6 | **4.** 245 ÷ 5 | **5.** 171 ÷ 9 | **6.** 168 ÷ 8

Explore It

Suppose you want to find 381 ÷ 4.
Can you use addition to help you divide?
Explain why or why not.

Teacher Notes

Explore: Add to Divide

Objective Use addition to find quotients.

Using the Explore (Activities to use after Lesson 1)

The model for division is splitting a collection into equal groups. In this activity, students explore a new way to think about division as splitting apart. They deconstruct division by using addition to find quotients. The critical thinking questions encourage students to look beyond a single solution. The Explore It asks students to apply their understanding to a new situation and explain their reasoning.

Math Journal You may wish to have students use their *Math Journals* for the Explore It.

Going Beyond Guide students to recognize that 381, from the Explore It, may be written as 380 + 1, and ask them to divide using addition. The quotient is 95, and the remainder is 1. You may wish to provide additional division exercises for students.

Solutions

$105 = 70 + 35$
$70 \div 7 = 10; 35 \div 7 = 5;$
$10 + 5 = 15$

1. $98 + 7; 91 + 14; 84 + 21;$
$77 + 28; 63 + 42; 56 + 49$

2. *Answers may vary. Sample:* Yes. I found all the addends of 105 that are divisible by 7. First I listed all the products that are less than 105 that have 7 as one of the factors. Then I matched the pairs of products that add up to 105.

3. 600, 54; *Answers may vary. Sample:*
$600 \div 6 = 100, 54 \div 6 = 9$
$100 + 9 = 109$

4. 200, 45
$200 \div 5 = 40, 45 \div 5 = 9$
$40 + 9 = 49$

5. 72, 99
$72 \div 9 = 8, 99 \div 9 = 11$
$8 + 11 = 19$

6. 160, 8
$160 \div 8 = 20, 8 \div 8 = 1$
$20 + 1 = 21$

Explore It You cannot use addition to find the quotient of $381 \div 4$, because you cannot write 381 as two addends divisible by 4. The quotient is 95 R1.

Division Around the World

Most students around the world learn how to divide.
Did you know that they use different ways to divide?

United States and Mexico	Brazil and Russia	Pakistan and The Netherlands
174 R2 3)524 − 3 22 − 21 14 − 12 2	524 ⌐3 − 3 174 R2 22 − 21 14 − 12 2	3 ⌐524 ⌐174 R2 − 3 22 − 21 14 − 12 2

1. Compare and Contrast How are the methods similar? _____

_____

How are they different? _____

_____

Write a different division exercise for each country. Find each quotient as if you were a student in that country.

2. Russia	**3.** Pakistan	**4.** Mexico	**5.** Brazil

6. Which method do you think is simplest to use? Why?

_____

Extend It

Make up a new method to find 524 ÷ 3.
Tell why your method should be taught in schools.

Teacher Notes

Extend: Division Around the World

Objective Divide 3-digit dividends by 1-digit divisors.

Using the Extend (Activities to use after Lesson 3)
Research indicates that students' linguistic and cultural experiences influence their understanding of mathematical algorithms. It is common in American classrooms to introduce ancient number systems as a way to expand this type of thinking. In this activity, students are challenged to compare division algorithms of different countries. The critical thinking questions prompt students to analyze the efficiency of the algorithms. The Extend It gives students an opportunity to develop their own division algorithm and justify the solution method they choose.

Math Journal You may wish to have students use their *Math Journals* for the Extend It.

Going Beyond Give students division exercises with 2-digit divisors and have them find the quotients using their method and methods from other countries.

Solutions

1. They are the same because all three methods use multiplication, then subtraction to divide. They are different because in each method, the quotient is written in a different place.

Answers may vary. Sample:

2. Russia

```
453 |2
 -4   226 R1
 05
 -4
 13
-12
  1
```

3. Pakistan

```
3 |136  45 R1
  - 12
    16
  - 15
     1
```

4. Mexico

```
  145 R1
5)726
 - 5
   22
 - 20
   26
 - 25
    1
```

5. Brazil

```
772 |3
 -6   257 R1
 17
-15
 22
-21
  1
```

6. *Answers may vary. Sample:* The first method is simplest. The digits in the quotient line up with the digits in the dividend.

Extend It *Answers may vary. Sample:* This method should be taught in schools because the dividend and quotient are lined up by place value. This makes it easier to tell which place you should divide.

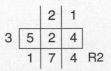

Math and the Solar System

Our solar system consists of the Sun, 9 planets, more than 100 satellites of the planets, many comets and asteroids, and the interplanetary medium, or space, between the planets.

A planet's path around the Sun is called its **orbit**. The length of the year on a planet is determined by the time it takes that planet to orbit the Sun.

The table at the right shows the planets in our solar system arranged in order from closest to the Sun to farthest from the Sun.

Use a calculator to solve these problems about the Solar System.

Length of Year	
Planet	**Orbit in Earth Days**
Mercury	88
Venus	225
Earth	365
Mars	687
Jupiter	4,333
Saturn	10,759
Uranus	30,685
Neptune	60,188
Pluto	90,700

1. About how many Earth years will it take Mars to orbit the Sun?

   How did you find the answer? _____

2. If Uranus begins its orbit around the Sun in 2007, in what Earth year

   will it complete the orbit? _____

3. Imagine that a satellite transmits photos of Neptune to Earth for $\frac{1}{2}$ of a Neptune year. For about how many Earth weeks will it transmit photos?

   _____

4. **Explain** Satellite A can transmit a photo of Neptune every 5 days for a full Neptune year. Satellite B can transmit a photo of Pluto every 8 days for a full Pluto year. Explain how you know that Satellite A can transmit more photos than Satellite B.

   _____

Connect It

Use the table to write division problems about the Solar System. Show the answers for your problems.

Teacher Notes

Connect: Math and the Solar System

Objective Solve multi-step word problems using division.
Materials calculator

Using the Connect (Activities to use after Lesson 5)

In this activity, students use data about planets' orbits to solve multi-step word problems. The problems are constructed to encourage students to explain their reasoning. The Connect It helps students synthesize their understanding by having them use the given data to create and solve their own word problems.

Math Journal You may wish to have students use their *Math Journals* for the Connect It.

Going Beyond Have students research further information about the Solar System. Ask them to create their own math worksheet using this information.

Solutions

1. about 2 years; I divided the number of days it takes Mars to orbit the Sun, 687, by the number of days in one Earth year, 365.

   $687 \div 365 = 1.88$, or about 2 years.

2. the year 2091

3. about 4,299 Earth weeks

4. *Answers may vary. Sample:*
   I can find the number of photos Satellite A transmits by dividing the length of the Neptune year, 60,188, by the frequency of transmission in days, 5. $60,188 \div 5 = 12,037.6$.

   Then I can find the number of photos Satellite B transmits by dividing the length of the Pluto year, 90,700, by the frequency of transmission in days, 8. $90,700 \div 8 = 11,337.5$

   $12,037.6 > 11,337.5$, so Satellite A transmits more photos.

Connect It *Answers may vary. Sample:*
If Maria is 9 years old in Earth years, about how old is she in Mars years?

First you multiply Maria's age on Earth, 9, by the number of days in one Earth year, 365. $9 \times 365 = 3,285$.
Then you divide 3,285 by the number of days in a Mars year, 687.
$3,285 \div 687 = 4.7$.
So, Maria is about 5 years old in Mars years.

Number Patterns

Did you know that multiples of certain numbers follow patterns?

The multiples of 2 are all even numbers.
The multiples of 10 all have 0 in the ones place.

Let's explore other patterns.

The following is a list of some of the multiples of 9.

9, 18, 27, 36, 45, 54, 63, 72, 81, 90

1. What pattern do you observe for each multiple of 9? _____

_____

_____

_____

2. Analyze Do you think 117 is a multiple of 9? Explain. _____

_____

_____

3. Look at the numbers shown below.
Write the numbers that are multiples of 9.

26   153   91   164   802   207   39   35   531

_____

4. Explain how you know which numbers in Exercise 3
are not multiples of 9. Give an example.

_____

Explore It

Use the pattern you discovered to answer these questions.
Is 648 a multiple of 9? Explain why or why not.
Is 7,064,235 a multiple of 9? Explain why or why not.

Teacher Notes

Explore: Number Patterns

Objective Find patterns using multiples.

Using the Explore (Activities to use after Lesson 1)
The "count on" strategy that students have used is linked to multiples. Finding patterns involving multiples and factors leads to a better understanding of multiplication and division. A critical thinking question helps students test the pattern they observed. The Explore It challenges students to use the pattern to determine if greater numbers, such as 648 and 7,064,235, are multiples of 9.

Math Journal You may wish to have students use their *Math Journals* for the Explore It activity.

Going Beyond Ask students to find patterns for other multiples. For example, they might find that the multiples of 5 have either 0 or 5 in the ones place.

Solutions

1. The sum of the digits of each multiple is equal to 9.
   18: 1 + 8 = 9
   27: 2 + 7 = 9
   36: 3 + 6 = 9
   45: 4 + 5 = 9
   54: 5 + 4 = 9
   63: 6 + 3 = 9
   72: 7 + 2 = 9
   81: 8 + 1 = 9
   90: 9 + 0 = 9

2. Yes. 117 is a multiple of 9, because 1 + 1 + 7 = 9.

3. 153, 207, and 531.

4. *Answers may vary. Sample:* If the sum of the digits in the number does not equal 9, the number is not a multiple of 9. For example, 2 + 6 = 8, so 26 is not a multiple of 9.

Explore It Yes. *Answers may vary. Sample:* Add the digits in 648.
6 + 4 + 8 = 18.
Add the digits in 18. 1 + 8 = 9.
So, 648 is a multiple of 9.

Yes. *Answers may vary. Sample:*
Add the digits in 7,064,235.
7 + 0 + 6 + 4 + 2 + 3 + 5 = 27.
Add the digits in 27. 2 + 7 = 9.
So, 7,064,235 is a multiple of 9.

Name _____   Date _____

Prime Number Theories

Do you think every even number greater than 2 can be written
as the sum of two prime numbers?

Let's try these.

$10 = 3 + 7$

$14 = 3 +$ _____

10 is an even number.
3 and 7 are prime numbers.

14 is an even number.

3 and _____ are prime numbers.

1. List 10 prime numbers. _____

_____

2. Write 20 sums that can be made using the prime numbers

you wrote. _____

_____

_____

_____

_____

3. Compare and Contrast Look at the sums you wrote. What is

your theory about the sum of prime numbers? _____

_____

Extend It

List 12 odd numbers that are prime numbers. Write 4 sums that
can be made using 3 of the prime numbers you wrote. What is
your theory about the sum of 3 prime numbers that are odd?

Teacher Notes

Extend: Prime Number Theories

Objective Explore prime numbers.

Using the Extend (Activities to use after Lesson 3)

This activity involves examining patterns for the sums of prime numbers. Many mathematicians have tried to find patterns involving prime numbers. Christian Goldbach was a professor of mathematics and historian at St. Petersburg in Russia. In 1742 he wrote a letter to Leonard Euler, a famous mathematician. In the letter Goldbach stated that every even number greater than 2 can be written as the sum of two prime numbers. His theory is known as the Goldbach Conjecture. Although no one has ever proven this idea completely, computers have proven that Goldbach's Conjecture is true up to one million. The critical thinking question leads students to Goldbach's Conjecture. The Extend It focuses on Goldbach's second theory, which states that every odd number greater than 7 can be written as the sum of 3 odd prime numbers.

Math Journal You may wish to have students use their *Math Journals* for the Extend It activity.

Going Beyond As the students write the prime numbers, ask them to note in their *Math Journals* any observations concerning prime numbers. Possible observations could be that 2 is the only prime even number and that as the numbers become greater, the distance between prime numbers increases.

Solutions

11; 11

1. *Answers may vary. Sample:* 3, 5, 7, 11, 13, 17, 19, 23, 29, 31

2. *Answers may vary. Sample:*
   $3 + 3 = 6$; $3 + 5 = 8$;
   $3 + 7 = 10$; $3 + 11 = 14$;
   $3 + 13 = 16$; $3 + 17 = 20$;
   $3 + 19 = 22$; $3 + 23 = 26$;
   $3 + 29 = 32$; $3 + 31 = 34$;
   $5 + 7 = 12$; $5 + 11 = 16$;
   $5 + 13 = 18$; $5 + 17 = 22$;
   $5 + 19 = 24$; $5 + 23 = 28$;
   $5 + 29 = 34$; $5 + 31 = 36$;
   $7 + 11 = 18$; $7 + 13 = 20$

3. *Answers may vary. Sample:* Every even number greater than 2 can be written as the sum of 2 prime numbers.

Extend It *Answers may vary. Sample:*
3, 5, 7, 11, 13, 17, 19, 23, 29, 31, 37, 41

$3 + 5 + 7 = 15$, $3 + 7 + 11 = 21$,
$5 + 7 + 13 = 25$, $13 + 17 + 23 = 53$;
The sum is always odd when you add 3 odd prime numbers.

Grade Averages

Ali	81	74	93	67	100
Chloe	90	61	75	85	94
Cliff	24	70	95	97	94
Heidi	54	76	100	96	84
Clyde	82	94	60	89	95

Teachers use averaging to determine report card grades and class rank. The grade book at the right shows the grades for a history class.

Use a calculator and the grade book to solve these problems.

1. Find the grade average for each student. Then rank these students' grade averages from highest average to lowest average.

_____

_____

2. What would happen to each student's grade average if the lowest grade is dropped before averaging?

_____

_____

3. **Analyze** How can the student having the lowest grade average on the 4 tests move up in class rank on the next test?

_____

_____

Connect It

Suppose you took 5 math tests and you have a grade average of 82. What grade do you need to get on the next test to raise your grade average to 85? Explain your answer.

Teacher Notes

Connect: Grade Averages

Objective Solve problems involving average.
Materials calculator

Using the Connect (Activities to use after Lesson 5)

In this activity, students use data from a chart to solve word problems that involve finding grade averages and class rank. The problems are constructed to encourage students to explore how grade averages can be changed by dropping grades, improving grades, and adding more grades. A critical thinking question asks students to analyze how a student can move up in class rank. It challenges students by having them manipulate data to answer the question. The Connect It challenges students to determine the grade needed on another test to reach a target grade average.

Math Journal You may wish to have students use their *Math Journals* for the Connect It activity.

Going Beyond Have students add 3 more grades to the 5 grades given for each student in the grade book. Then have them find the new average and class rank.

Solutions

1. Clyde: 84, Ali: 83, Heidi: 82, Chloe: 81, and Cliff: 76

2. *Answers may vary. Sample:* Dropping the lowest score will raise each student's average.

3. *Answers may vary. Sample:* If Chloe receives a grade of 100 on the next test and everyone else receives a grade of 83 or less, Chloe's class rank will change from last place to first place.

Connect It I would need to get a grade of 100 on the next test to reach an average grade of 85 on the 6 tests. *Answers may vary. Sample:* The sum of the grades on the 5 tests must be 410 to have a grade average of 82 on the 5 tests since $82 \times 5 = 410$. The sum of the grades on the 6 tests would need to be 510 to have a grade average of 85 on the 6 tests since $85 \times 6 = 510$. $510 - 410 = 100$.

Two in One

This function machine combines two
operations into a single machine.

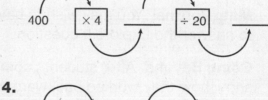

Look at the rules.

The first rule is × 3. The second rule is _____.

The first input is 1,000. The second input is _____.

The final output is _____.

Complete these function machines.

1.
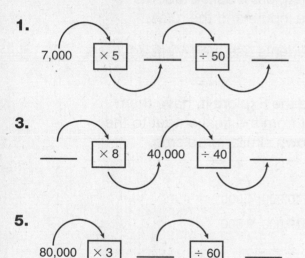

2.
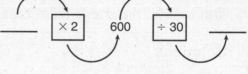

3.

4.

5.

6.

7. **Analyze** Write the rules in the boxes.

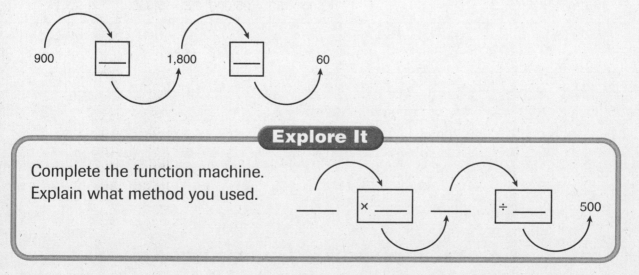

Explore It

Complete the function machine.
Explain what method you used.

Teacher Notes

Explore: Two in One

Objective Complete two-operation function machines.

Using the Explore (Activities to use after Lesson 1)
In this activity, students multiply by multiples of 10, 100, and 1,000 and divide by multiples of 10, 100, and 1,000 in order to complete two-operation function machines. More challenging exercises involve missing factors, while others involve multiples of 10,000. The critical thinking question asks students to supply the rules for a two-operation function machine. The Explore It asks students to work backward from a final output to the inputs and the rules.

Math Journal You may wish to have students use their *Math Journals* to answer the Explore It question.

Going Beyond After students complete the Explore It, have them show how they worked backward to get from the final output to the first input. Then have them create their own similar problems.

Solutions

÷ 50
3,000
60

1. 35,000; 700

2. 1,600; 80

3. 5,000; 1,000

4. 300; 20

5. 240,000; 4,000

6. 810,000; 9,000

7. × 2; ÷ 30

Explore It *Answers may vary.*
Sample: 5,000; 5; 25,000; 50.
I used working backward and inverse operations:
500 × 50 = 25,000 ÷ 5 = 5,000.

Calorie Count

The chart below shows the number of calories used by a 130-pound person in 1 hour when he or she paddles a canoe, rides a mountain bike, or does other activities.

You can estimate to find the number of calories a person uses in 1 minute. When you estimate, you do not need to find the exact amount. You can find about how many calories a person uses in 1 minute.

A person paddling a canoe uses 236 calories in 1 hour. Divide the number of calories used in 1 hour by the number of minutes in 1 hour. Use compatible numbers to divide.

$236 \div 60 \rightarrow 240 \div 60 = 4$
Paddling a canoe uses about 4 calories in 1 minute.

> 1 hour = 60 minutes

> Compatible numbers are easy to divide.

Complete the chart for the other activities.

	Activity	Calories Used by 130-pound Person in 1 Hour	Estimate of Calories Used in 1 Minute
	Canoeing	236	4
1.	Mountain biking	502	
2.	Skateboarding	295	
3.	Playing basketball	472	
4.	Sledding	413	
5.	Rope jumping	590	

Extend It

For each activity, estimate the number of calories a person uses in 15 minutes, in 30 minutes, and in 45 minutes.

Teacher Notes

Extend: Calorie Count

Objective Estimate calories used in 1 minute given calories used in 1 hour.

Using the Extend (Activities to use after Lesson 3)
In this activity, students use data in a chart and compatible numbers to divide in order to make estimates. The Extend It has students use their estimation skills in order to generate more data.

Math Journal You may wish to have students use their *Math Journals* for the Extend It activity.

Going Beyond Have students compare the data from the Extend It. For example: Does a person use more calories rope jumping for 15 minutes or canoeing for 30 minutes? The answer is rope jumping for 15 minutes. Then have students look up similar data for their favorite activities and display the data in a chart like the one used in this activity.

Solutions

Estimates may vary for Exercises 1–5. Samples:

1. $480 \div 60 = 8$

2. $300 \div 60 = 5$

3. $480 \div 60 = 8$

4. $420 \div 60 = 7$

5. $600 \div 60 = 10$

Extend It *Answers may vary. Samples:*
Canoeing: 15 min: 60; 30 min: 120; 45 min: 180

Mountain biking: 15 min: 120; 30 min: 240; 45 min: 360

Skateboarding: 15 min: 75; 30 min: 150; 45 min: 225

Basketball game: 15 min: 120; 30 min: 240; 45 min: 360

Sledding: 15 min: 105; 30 min: 210; 45 min: 315

Rope jumping: 15 min: 150; 30 min: 300; 45 min: 450

Casting Out Nines

You can check that 392 ÷ 14 = 28 by multiplying: 14 × 28 = 392.
You can even check that your multiplication is correct.

Step 1: Add the digits in 14 until you have a single digit. $1 + 4 = 5$	**Step 2:** Add the digits in 28 until you have a single digit. $2 + 8 = 10$ and $1 + 0 = 1$.
Step 3: Multiply the two sums from Step 1 and Step 2. $5 × 1 = 5$	**Step 4:** Add the digits in 392 until you have a single digit. $3 + 9 + 2 = 14$ and $1 + 4 = 5$.

The sum in Step 3 equals the sum in Step 4. 5 = 5.

If your number sentence is correct, these two sums will always be equal. If your number sentence is not correct, these two sums could still be equal.

You can make the addition of the digits easier by "casting out nines."
Look at Step 1. There is no 9 to subtract or "cast out."
Look at Step 2. If you cast out 9, then $10 - 9 = 1$.
Look at Step 4. If you cast out 9, then $14 - 9 = 5$.

Find each quotient. Check by using the method on this page.

1. 989 ÷ 23   **2.** 1,525 ÷ 25   **3.** 8,342 ÷ 97   **4.** 2,268 ÷ 63

_____   _____   _____   _____

5. Analyze What if you have a remainder? Find 427 ÷ 26.

_____

Connect It

On a separate sheet of paper, add 3 four-digit numbers. Use the "casting out nines" method to check the addition.

Teacher Notes

Connect: Casting Out Nines

Objective Check division using multiplication and the "casting out nines" method.

Using the Connect (Activities to use after Lesson 5)
In this activity, students find two-digit quotients. Then they use the casting out nines method when multiplying to check their division. The casting out nines method is thought to have come from India. It dates back to 1478. The critical thinking question tests students' understanding of the remainder in division. The Connect It asks students to apply the method of casting out nines they used when checking multiplication to addition.

Math Journal You may wish to have students use their *Math Journals* for the Connect It activity.

Going Beyond Help students cast out nines as they check the addition in the Connect It. They should notice that the method works in the same way for addition as it does for multiplication. When they have finished the Connect It, encourage them to try even greater numbers.

Solutions

1. 43; Check:

$$
\begin{array}{ccc}
23 & \longrightarrow & 5 \\
\underline{\times 43} & \longrightarrow & \underline{\times 7} \\
989 \rightarrow 8 & & 35 \rightarrow 8
\end{array}
$$

$$8 = 8$$

2. 61; Check:

$$
\begin{array}{ccc}
25 & \longrightarrow & 7 \\
\underline{\times 61} & \longrightarrow & \underline{\times 7} \\
1{,}525 \rightarrow 4 & & 49 \rightarrow 4
\end{array}
$$

$$4 = 4$$

3. 86; Check:

$$
\begin{array}{ccc}
97 & \longrightarrow & 7 \\
\underline{\times 86} & \longrightarrow & \underline{\times 5} \\
8{,}342 \rightarrow 8 & & 35 \rightarrow 8
\end{array}
$$

$$8 = 8$$

4. 36; Check:

$$
\begin{array}{ccc}
63 & \longrightarrow & 0 \\
\underline{\times 36} & \longrightarrow & \underline{\times 0} \\
2{,}268 \rightarrow 0 & & 0
\end{array}
$$

$$0 = 0$$

5. 16 R11. *Answers may vary. Sample:*
Before you multiply to check, subtract the remainder from the dividend. Then use that number as your product.

Check: First subtract:
427 − 11 = 416. Then:

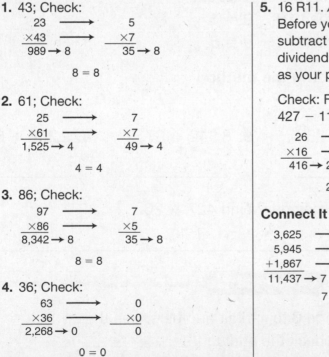

$$
\begin{array}{ccc}
26 & \longrightarrow & 8 \\
\underline{\times 16} & \longrightarrow & \underline{\times 7} \\
416 \rightarrow 2 & & 56 \rightarrow 2
\end{array}
$$

$$2 = 2$$

Connect It *Answers may vary. Sample:*

$$
\begin{array}{ccc}
3{,}625 & \longrightarrow & 7 \\
5{,}945 & \longrightarrow & 5 \\
\underline{+1{,}867} & \longrightarrow & \underline{+4} \\
11{,}437 \rightarrow 7 & & 16 \rightarrow 7
\end{array}
$$

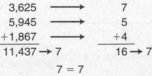

$$7 = 7$$

Egyptian Measures

Before there were standard units such as inches and feet,
people used body measures. The ancient Egyptians used
cubits, palms, and digits to measure length.

• A cubit is the length from your elbow to the tips of your fingers.
• A palm is the width of your hand.
• A digit is the width of your finger.

What unit of measure do you think an Egyptian would use to measure each length?

a serving tray _____   a small boat _____   a bean _____

1. Measure 3 objects in your classroom in cubits, palms, and digits.
   Use the table below to record the length of each object.

Object	Length in Cubits	Length in Palms	Length in Digits

2. **Analyze** Explain how two people could measure the same
   object but find different lengths using Egyptian measures.

   _____

3. Here is how cubits, palms, and digits are related.
       1 cubit = 7 palms   1 palm = 4 digits
   Imagine you have a robe that is 3 cubits long.

   Think
   Should I multiply
   or divide?

   How long is the robe in palms? _____

   How long is the robe in digits? _____

Explore It

Look at the objects in your chart. Check each object's length in
cubits. Find each object's length in palms and digits using the
conversions in Exercise 3. Compare these measurements to
the measurements in your table. Are they the same?

Teacher Notes

Explore: Egyptian Measures

Objective Use Egyptian units of measurement to measure length.

Using the Explore (Activities to use after Lesson 1)

In this activity, students work with units of measurement used by the ancient Egyptians to find the length of objects in the classroom. They also make conversions among units in the Egyptian system. The critical thinking question emphasizes the need for a standard unit of measure. The Explore It furthers this concept by comparing the measurements they found to measurements derived using conversions.

Math Journal You may wish to have students use their *Math Journals* for the Explore It.

Going Beyond Explain to students that the length of cubits, palms, and digits were later standardized to exact amounts. Have students explain the differences between using the Egyptian measures and a standardized method of measurement.

Solutions

Serving tray—palm
Small boat—cubit
Bean—digit

1. *Answers may vary. Check students' charts.*

2. *Answers may vary. Sample:* A cubit for a short person would be smaller than a cubit for a large person. They would find different measures for the same objects.

3. 21 palms; 84 digits

Explore It *Answers may vary. Check students' work.*

Missing Units

Sometimes when you convert measurements, you need to find the missing unit of measure.

Alfonso has 3 gallons of juice. He pours the juice in 12 containers so that there is an equal amount of juice in each container. How much juice is in each container?

Think
12 is 4 times greater than 3. 1 gallon is 4 times greater than 1 quart.

Solution: There is 1 quart of juice in each container.

Try another example.

3 yards = 9 _____

Find the missing units of measure.

1. 3 pt = 6 _____

2. 12 ft = 4 _____

3. 5 _____ = 20 qt

4. 48 _____ = 4 ft

5. 16 qt = 4 _____

6. 6 _____ = 72 in.

7. 3,520 yd = 2 _____

8. 15,840 _____ = 3 mi

9. Explain Sometimes both units of measure are missing.

Solve the following problem: 5 _____ = 60 _____.

Explain how you found your answer. _____

_____

_____

Extend It

Look at the following problem: 4 _____ = 2 _____.
Is there more than one answer to this problem?
Explain your thinking.

Teacher Notes

Extend: Missing Units

Objective Compare equivalent measures to find missing units of measure.

Using the Extend (Activities to use after Lesson 3)
In this activity, students are presented with equivalent measures with one of the units missing. Students will need to recall what they know about relationships between units of length and between units of capacity in order to write the missing unit. The critical thinking question challenges students to find two missing units. The Extend It has students look beyond a single solution.

Math Journal You may wish to have students use their *Math Journals* for the Extend It.

Going Beyond Have students create their own word problems in which missing units of measure must be found.

Solutions

3 yards = 9 feet

1. c

2. yd

3. gal

4. in.

5. gal

6. ft

7. mi

8. ft

9. ft; in. *Explanations may vary. Sample:* 60 is equal to 12 times 5. One foot is 12 times longer than 1 inch, so 5 feet is equal to 60 inches.

Extend It *Answers may vary. Sample:* Yes. 4 cups is equal to 2 pints. 4 pints is equal to 2 quarts.

Name _____ Date _____

Estimating Measurements

Jen is picking blueberries at a farm. She picks 19 cups of berries in all. When she is finished, the farmer asks her about how many quarts she has. What should she tell the farmer?

Step 1: Change cups to quarts. Remember, 1 c = 4 qt. You are changing to a larger unit, so divide. $19 \div 4 = 4\ R3$ or 4 quarts with 3 cups left over	**Step 2:** Round the number of quarts to estimate. 3 cups is about 1 quart, so add another quart to estimate. $4 + 1 = 5$

Solution: Jen should tell the farmer she has about 5 quarts.

Estimate each missing number.

1. _____ pints in 45 cups

2. _____ gallons in 23 quarts

3. _____ yards in 31 feet

4. _____ pounds in 56 ounces

5. _____ miles in 6,000 yards

Think
$45 \div 2 = 22\ R1$
1 cup is halfway between 22 pints and 23 pints so round up.

6. **Analyze** Jen is paying for the berries. If Jen tells the farmer the exact number of berries she has instead of an estimate, will the amount she pays change? Explain.

_____

_____

Connect It

Give examples of when you would need to use an exact measurement. Then give examples of when you could use an estimated measurement.

Teacher Notes

Connect: Estimating Measurements

Objective Convert and round measurements to estimate amounts.

Using the Connect (Activities to use after Lesson 5)
In this activity, students convert customary units of length, capacity, and weight, then round these measurements in order to estimate amounts. The critical thinking question focuses on whether an estimate is appropriate for a situation or whether an exact answer is necessary. The Connect It asks students to provide examples of when they would estimate and when they need an exact measurement.

Math Journal You may wish to have students use their *Math Journals* to answer the Connect It question.

Going Beyond Have students create their own conversion exercises where rounding is necessary.

Solutions

1. about 23 pints

2. about 6 gallons

3. about 10 yards

4. about 4 pounds

5. about 3 miles

6. *Answers may vary. Sample:* Yes. If Jen pays an exact amount, she will pay less because when she estimated, she rounded up.

Connect It *Answers may vary. Sample:* You would need to use an exact measurement for a dose of medicine. You could estimate the distance between two houses.

Calendar Conversions

You know how old you are in years. But have you ever wondered how old you are in months or days? Complete the chart below. You can use a calendar if you need to.

	In Years	In Months	In Days
My Age Today			

1. How did you calculate your age in days?

_____

2. Analyze Which answers were affected by including leap years in

your calculations? Why? _____

_____

About how old will you be when you graduate from 12th grade? Assume that you will graduate on May 31. Complete the chart below.

	In Years	In Months	In Days
My Age when I Graduate from 12th Grade			

3. Explain How could you calculate your graduation age in hours?

_____

_____

Explore It

Mathew is 11 years old today. Gina is 3,834 days old and DeVine is 138 months old. On a separate sheet of paper, order the students' ages from youngest to oldest and explain how you know.

Teacher Notes

Explore: Calendar Conversions

Objective Convert years to months and days.

Using the Explore (Activities to use after Lesson 1)
Students must use a combination of computations and logical reasoning to find their ages in months and in days. Make sure they consider the leap years 1996, 2000, 2004, 2008, and 2012 in their calculations. The problems are designed so that students may take several approaches to the solutions. Encourage them to explain their reasoning in clear, concise language. The Explore It asks students to solve a logical reasoning problem.

Math Journal You may wish to have students use their *Math Journals* to answer the Explore It question.

Going Beyond Have students use a calculator to find their age in minutes. Ask them to explain their calculations. They should recognize that there are 24 hours in a day and 60 minutes in an hour.

Solutions

Answers may vary. Sample answer for a student born on 1/8/95 and is calculating his or her age on 3/11/05:

Years	Months	Days
10	122	3,715

1. *Answers may vary. Sample:* My birth date is 1/8/95 and today is 3/11/05. To calculate my age in days, I multiplied 10 years times 365 to get 3,650 days. Then I added 3 days for the leap years 1996, 2000, and 2004 to get 3,653 days. Then I added 31 days for the month from 1/8/05 to 2/8/05 and 28 days for the month from 2/8/05 to 3/8/05. Finally, I added 3 more days to get a total of 3,715 days.

2. *Answers may vary. Sample:* Only the age in days is affected by leap years, because a leap year adds 1 day to the length of a year. The number of years and months stays the same.

Answers may vary. Sample answer for a student born on 1/8/95 and graduating on 5/31/13:

Years	Months	Days
18	220	6,718

3. *Answers may vary. Sample:* There are 24 hours in a day. I found how old I am in days. So, I could multiply the number of days times 24 to find how many hours.

Explore It *Answers may vary. Sample:* From youngest to oldest, the order is: Gina, Mathew, DeVine. To solve the problem, I compared the students' ages by years. Mathew is 11 years old. I divided 3,834 by 365 days to find that Gina is about $10\frac{1}{2}$ years old. I divided 138 by 12 months to find that DeVine is $11\frac{1}{2}$ years old.

Time Zones

Carlos is flying west from Baltimore, Maryland, to Denver, Colorado. The table shows the flights he can take. He will have to make a stop at another city along the way.

Trip	Time of Departure	Flight 1 Length	Layover Length	Flight 2 Length	Total Trip Length
A	9:00 A.M.	2 hours 3 minutes	1 hour 58 minutes	1 hour 38 minutes	
B	10:20 A.M.	2 hours 17 minutes	43 minutes	2 hours 25 minutes	
C	8:45 A.M.	2 hours 2 minutes	1 hour 28 minutes	2 hours 36 minutes	

1. Complete the table by calculating the total time for each trip.

2. Which trip takes the least amount of time? _____

   Which takes the greatest amount of time? _____

When traveling west across time zones, subtract one hour for each time zone crossed. When traveling east, add one hour for each time zone. Carlos will cross two time zones.

3. **Analyze** Which flight has the earliest arrival in Denver? What time will it arrive? Explain.

   _____

4. Does the shortest flight arrive earliest in Denver? Why or why not?

   _____

Extend It

Suppose Carlos' mother is planning a business trip. When she travels west from Baltimore to Denver, should she schedule a morning or afternoon meeting in Denver? When she travels east from Denver to Baltimore, should she schedule a morning or afternoon meeting in Baltimore? On a separate sheet of paper, explain your reasoning.

Teacher Notes

Extend: Time Zones

Objective Solve multi-step elapsed time problems.

Using the Extend (Activities to use after Lesson 3)

In this activity, students solve real-world, multi-step elapsed time problems that require them to consider time zones. The problems are designed so that students may choose different approaches to the solution. For these problems, in addition to finding the answer, students must also explain their computation. The Extend It asks students to apply what they learned about traveling across time zones.

Math Journal You may wish to have students use their *Math Journals* to answer the Extend It question.

Going Beyond Have students research information about flights from the closest airport in their city to cities in other states and Europe. Ask them to create their own problems using this information.

Solutions

1. Flight A: 5 hours 39 minutes
   Flight B: 5 hours 25 minutes
   Flight C: 6 hours 6 minutes

2. B; C

3. Flight A; it will arrive in Denver at 12:39 P.M. *Answers may vary. Sample:* I added all of the flying time and layover time together for each flight. Then I added the total time to the time of departure. Finally, I subtracted two hours for the two time zones that Carlos crossed to find the arrival time.

4. No. *Answers may vary. Sample:* Flight A is the flight that gets to Denver the earliest, but it is not the shortest flight. The shortest flight leaves much later in the morning.

Extend It *Answers may vary. Sample:* Since Carlos' mother gains two hours on the trip west, she can easily arrive for a morning meeting. Since she loses two hours on the trip east, she should probably schedule an afternoon meeting, or else travel the night before to arrive in time for a morning meeting.

A Temperature Experiment

Not all liquids are the same. Water flows easily, while corn syrup is thick and flows slowly. As temperature rises, some liquids get thicker and some liquids get thinner. The experiment below shows how temperature affects the thickness of corn syrup.

To do the experiment, a glass cylinder was filled with corn syrup. Two marks were made on the cylinder. The temperature of the corn syrup was measured. Then a steel ball was dropped into the liquid. The scientist used a stop watch to see how long it took the ball to fall from one mark to the other.

The Results are shown on the table below.

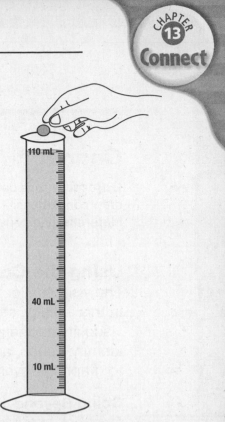

| Temperature | Time (to the nearest second) | | | | | Average Time |
	Trial 1	Trial 2	Trial 3	Trial 4	Trial 5	
10°C	80	42	67	50	71	
24°C	8	8	7	9	8	
47°C	2	2	2	2	2	
60°C	1	1	1	1	1	

1. Complete the table by finding the average time for each temperature.

2. What pattern do you notice in the data? _____

_____

3. **Interpret** Do you think the corn syrup gets thicker or thinner as the

   temperature increases? Explain. _____

4. **Predict** Suppose you drop a steel ball in corn syrup that has been heated to 70°C? What do you predict will happen? Explain.

_____

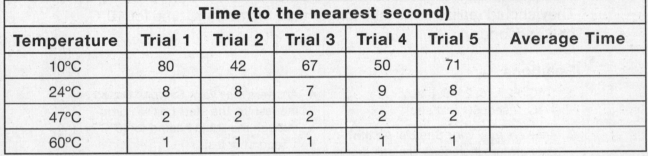

Connect It

On grid paper, graph the average time for each temperature shown.

Teacher Notes

Connect: A Temperature Experiment

Objective Use data on temperature changes to identify patterns and draw conclusions.
Materials grid paper

Using the Connect (Activities to use after Lesson 5)
The viscosity, or thickness, of most liquids is affected by temperature. In this activity, students interpret the results of an experiment on viscosity and temperature. Based on the data, they draw conclusions, identify trends, and make predictions. The Connect It asks students to graph the average results for each temperature.

Going Beyond Have students predict how long it would take the steel ball to fall from one mark to the other, if the corn syrup was 5°C. They should realize it will take longer than the average time for 10°C, or 62 seconds.

Solutions

1. 10°C: 62 sec; 24°C: 8 sec; 47°C: 2 sec; 60°C: 1 sec

2. *Answers may vary. Sample:* As the temperature increases, the ball drops faster; as the temperature decreases, the ball drops slower.

3. *Answers may vary. Sample:* As the temperature increases, the data shows that the ball moves quickly through the liquid. Thus, as the temperature increases, the corn syrup becomes less thick.

4. *Answers may vary. Sample:* Based on the results, the steel ball will drop through the liquid heated to 70°C in 1 second or less.

Connect It *Answers may vary. Check students' graphs.* Students should create a bar or line graph. Time should be labeled on the *y*-axis and Temperature should be labeled on the *x*-axis. Check that students have used correct intervals.

Number Cube Patterns

You can use a tally chart to record and organize data.

Roll a number cube 30 times. Tally how many times you roll each number in the chart.

Number	Tally	Frequency (number of occurrences)
1		
2		
3		
4		
5		
6		

On a separate sheet of paper, make two more tally charts. Repeat the activity two more times.

1. **Compare and Contrast** Compare the three tally charts. How are

   they alike? How are they different? _____

   _____

2. **Predict** Suppose you rolled the number cube 30 more times.

   What do you predict will happen? _____

On a separate sheet of paper, make another tally chart to test your prediction. Throw the number cube 30 more times and tally the results.

3. **Analyze** Based on this experiment, what conclusions can you draw
   about the chance of any number turning up on the number cube?

   _____

(Explore It)

Look at your data. Can you use it to predict which number will
turn up next? Explain why or why not.

Teacher Notes

Explore: Number Cube Patterns

Objective Organize and interpret data.
Materials number cube

Using the Explore (Activities to use after Lesson 1)

Students collect data on a tally chart to make predictions about the frequency of an event occurring. They roll a number cube and tally the frequency with which each number appears. Critical thinking questions lead them to interpret and make predictions from the data. The Explore It asks students to consider the limits of their data in making predictions.

Math Journal You may wish to have students use their *Math Journals* to answer the Explore It question.

Going Beyond Explain to students that the chance of any number on the cube turning up is 1 out of 6, or $\frac{1}{6}$. Have them compare their data for each number to this fraction.

Solutions

1. *Answers may vary. Sample:* Alike: three tally charts show that the numbers turned up with about the same frequency. Different: On one chart the numbers 1 and 2 turned up most often, while on another chart the numbers 3 and 6 occurred most often.

2. *Answers may vary. Sample:* I predict that all 6 numbers will turn up in about equal amounts.

3. *Answers may vary. Sample:* There is an equal chance of any one number turning up when the number cube is rolled. Some students may realize that the probability for each number is 1 out of 6, or $\frac{1}{6}$.

Explore It *Answers may vary. Sample:* No. My data shows that all six numbers have about the same chance of turning up with each throw of the number cube. Therefore, I can't use my data to predict which number will turn up.

Data Challenge

Ms. Gilmore found test score averages for some of the
students. This table shows the scores for each test and the
averages. Some of the scores are missing. Use the clues and
your knowledge of mean, median, mode, and range to find
the missing scores. You can use a calculator if you wish.

Name	Scores					Average (mean)
Talia		98	91		94	92
Abdul	80	83			88	85
Jeanette	76	79		71		79
Paul		95	88		96	92
Lamont	95		87		98	95

Clues

- The median of Abdul's test scores is 84.
- The mode of Paul's test scores is 88.
- The range of Talia's test scores is 13.
- The mode of Lamont's test scores is the same as his mean
  test score.
- The range of Jeanette's test scores is 1 more than the range
  of Talia's scores.

1. Explain how you found Abdul's test scores. _____

_____

2. **Analyze** How did knowing the range of the test scores help you

   find Jeanette's missing scores? _____

_____

_____

Extend It

Make up a problem with missing data that can be solved using the
mean, median, range, and/or mode of the data. Solve your problem.

Teacher Notes

Extend: Data Challenge

Objective Use logical reasoning to find the mean, median, mode, and range of a set of data.

Materials calculator (optional)

Using the Extend (Activities to use after Lesson 3)

In this activity, students must use logical reasoning and their knowledge of mean, median, mode, and range to find missing data. The focus of the activity is problem solving, so encourage students to use calculators to make any necessary calculations. Critical thinking questions prompt students to analyze their solution strategies. The Extend It encourages students to create their own problem.

Math Journal You may wish to have students use their *Math Journals* to answer the Extend It question.

Going Beyond Have students choose one student's data in the table. Have them change the student's average test score by several points, and then explain how it changes the missing data.

Solutions

Name	Scores					Average (mean)
Talia	[85]	98	91	[92]	94	92
Abdul	80	83	[90]	[84]	88	85
Jeanette	76	79	[84]	71	[85]	79
Paul	[88]	95	88	[93]	96	92
Lamont	95	[100]	87	[95]	98	95

1. *Answers may vary. Sample:* Abdul's median test score was 84. Since there were five test scores in all, the median score must be the middle score. This tells me that 84 is one of Abdul's missing scores. Once I knew that, I multiplied his average score by 5 to get the total: $5 \times 85 = 425$. Then I subtracted the other four scores to get the other missing score: $425 - 80 - 83 - 84 - 88 = 90$.

2. *Answers may vary. Sample:* The range is the difference between the greatest and least test scores. Knowing the range told me that one of Jeanette's scores was 14 more or less than 71, and when I tried to find the other missing score, I found that it needed to be 14 more than 71.

Extend It *Problems may vary but will be similar to the problems in this activity.*

Math and Architecture

One way to "see" the skyline of a city mathematically is to
make a stem-and-leaf plot of the heights of the city's buildings.
The data below shows the heights of the 20 tallest buildings
in Dallas, Texas. Use the data to make a stem-and-leaf plot.
Place the hundreds on the stem and the tens and ones on the
leaf. Hint: Remember to start by ordering
the data from least to greatest.

Stem	Leaves

**Heights of the 20
Tallest Buildings in Dallas, TX**
560 ft, 625 ft, 481 ft, 512 ft,
550 ft, 560 ft, 602 ft, 579 ft,
629 ft, 598 ft, 655 ft, 645 ft,
686 ft, 720 ft, 580 ft, 738 ft,
483 ft, 886 ft, 787 ft, 921 ft

1. Describe the shape of the stem-and-leaf plot. _____

_____

2. **Interpret** Do you expect the median height to be in

the 700–900 range? Explain. _____

_____

3. Explain how to find the median for this set of data. _____

_____

4. **Analyze** Suppose a new building is built in Dallas that is 886 feet tall.
   How would that affect the range? the median? the mode? Explain.

_____

_____

Connect It

Explain when you might want to plot data using a stem-and-leaf plot.

Teacher Notes

Connect: Math and Architecture

Objective Display data using a stem-and-leaf plot.

Using the Connect (Activities to use after Lesson 5)
In this activity, students extend the stem-and-leaf plot to data that is reported with numbers in the hundreds. They use real data to make a stem-and-leaf plot of building heights, then use the plot to answer questions. Critical thinking questions prompt students to interpret the data. The Connect It encourages students to consider when to use a stem-and-leaf plot.

Math Journal You may wish to have students use their *Math Journals* to answer the Connect It question.

Going Beyond Have students use a recent *World Almanac and Book of Facts* to find the 20 tallest buildings in a nearby city. Have them decide how to best show the data (bar graph, line plot, stem-and-leaf plot). Then ask them to plot the data using the graphic of their choice.

Solutions

Stem	Leaves
4	81 83
5	12 50 60 60 79 80 98
6	2 25 29 45 55 86
7	20 38 87
8	86
9	21

1. *Answers may vary. Sample:* The greatest number of leaves is on the 500 and 600 stems. There are only a few buildings taller and shorter than those.

2. No. *Answers may vary. Sample:* The median is the middle number, so it cannot be in the 700–900 range, as there are only 5 leaves on these stems, and 20 pieces of data altogether.

3. *Answers may vary. Sample:* The leaves are in order from least to greatest, so I can find the sum of the two middle numbers and divide by 2.

4. The range would not be affected, since the new building's height falls between the tallest and shortest buildings that already exist. The median would change to 625. There would be two modes—886 and 560.

Connect It *Answers may vary. Sample:* I would use a stem-and-leaf plot when I want to "see" data; a stem-and-leaf plot is like a bar graph made of numbers. I might also use one to find the data's median, mode, and range.

Averages and Bar Graphs

Jeff is making a double bar graph. The graph must show the
Ants' average runs scored per game and their opponents'
average runs scored per game for 4 weeks.

Here is the data he has collected so far.

Week 1 Runs Scored	
Ants	Opponents
6	4
3	2
1	2
1	3
4	5
3	8

Each row represents one game.

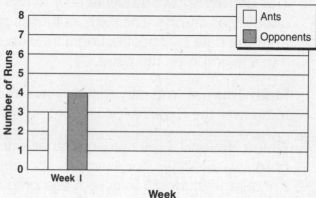

ANTS' AND OPPONENTS'
AVERAGE RUNS SCORED

1. **Analyze** How did Jeff use the data to make the bar graph?

_____

_____

2. Complete the double bar graph using the data below.

Week 2 Runs Scored	
Ants	Opponents
7	2
5	6
6	2
9	0
3	1
6	1

Week 3 Runs Scored	
Ants	Opponents
1	3
9	5
4	6
7	5
5	8
4	3

Week 4 Runs Scored	
Ants	Opponents
5	6
1	4
7	5
6	4
9	3
8	2

Explore It

Make a double bar graph to show how many games the Ants won per
week and how many games their opponents won per week. Compare
this graph to the graph on this page. How are they similar? Explain.

Teacher Notes

Explore: Averages and Bar Graphs

Objective Create and analyze double bar graphs that use averages.

Using the Explore (Activities to use after Lesson 1)

Students have learned how to find averages in a previous chapter. This activity shows students how to use averages to create their own double bar graphs. The Explore It asks students to draw conclusions from the data by constructing a new double bar graph and comparing it to the graph on the page.

Math Journal You may wish to have students use their *Math Journals* to answer the Explore It question.

Going Beyond Give students other examples of finding and graphing averages, for example, sports statistics and weather data. Encourage students to collect and graph their own data using a double bar graph.

Solutions

1. *Answers may vary. Sample:* First he added to find the total number of runs scored by the Ants during Week 1 and got 18. He divided 18 by the number of games played during Week 1, 6, to find the average, 3. Next, he added to find the total number of runs scored by the Opponents during Week 1 and got 24. He divided 24 by the number of games played during Week 1, 6, to find the average, 4.

2.

ANTS' AND OPPONENTS'
AVERAGE RUNS SCORED

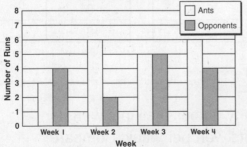

Explore It

ANTS' AND OPPONENTS' WINS
WINS PER WEEK

Answers may vary. Sample: The bar heights for both graphs look very similar. This is because the team that scores more runs per game will win more often.

Changing the Scale

If you use a different scale to graph the same data, the graphs can be interpreted differently.

Both these graphs show the number of visitors to the town of Centerville during September, October, November, and December.

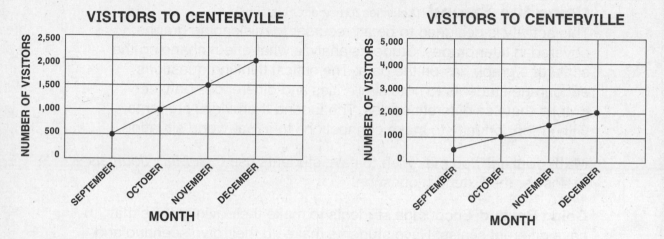

1. Observe How are the graphs similar? How are they different?

_____

_____

The bar graph at the right shows the number of stores in different towns. Look at the scale used in this graph.

On separate sheets of paper, draw similar bar graphs about the number of stores in different towns.

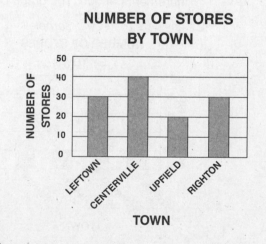

2. Draw one graph that uses a greater scale.

3. Draw one graph that uses a lesser scale.

Extend It

Look at the graphs you drew. How do the different scales change how you interpret the data? Which graph should the mayor of Upfield use to promote the number of stores in Upfield? Explain.

Teacher Notes

Extend: Changing the Scale

Objective Examine how changing the scale of a graph affects the visual interpretation of the data.

Using the Extend (Activities to use after Lesson 3)

This activity is designed to be a precursor to misleading graphs, covered in later grades. Students analyze what effect changing the scale of a graph has on the data. The critical thinking questions encourage students to note similarities and differences between graphs that use different scales. The Extend It provides students with an opportunity to make connections to a real-world situation.

Math Journal You may wish to have students use their *Math Journals* to answer the Extend It question.

Going Beyond Encourage students to make their own graphs that have different scales. Have students make up their own scenario and explain how the graphs can be interpreted differently.

Solutions

1. *Answers may vary. Sample:* Both graphs show the same data. They are different because the graphs have different scales. The graph on the left has a scale with increments of 500. The graph on the right has a scale with increments of 1,000.

2. *Answers may vary. Sample:*   3. *Answers may vary. Sample:*

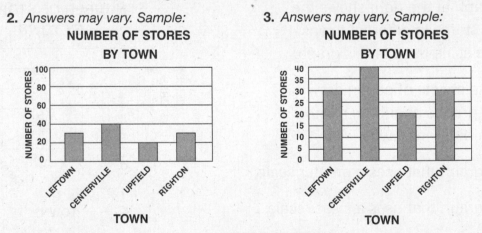

Extend It *Answers may vary. Sample:* The scale with lesser increments makes it appear that there is a large difference between the number of stores in the different towns. The scale with greater increments makes it appear that there is only a small difference between the number of stores in the different towns. The mayor of Upfield should use the graph with the greater scale because it makes it appear that there are about the same number of stores in each town.

Graphing a Report

Sometimes you are given a lot of information that needs to be displayed in graphs. Read this report about Marie's Music Store.

Sales are great at Marie's Music Store! We sold 30 instruments in January. We sold 10 fewer instruments in February. In March, however, we sold twice what we sold in February. We also did a survey in March. We learned that $\frac{1}{2}$ of our customers like guitars best and $\frac{1}{8}$ of our customers like pianos best. The rest of our customers like drums best. We had our best sales month in April, when we sold twice as many instruments as we did in January!

On a separate sheet of paper, use this report to make two different graphs. Use all of the information in the report for your graphs.

1. **Explain** How did you decide which graphs to use? _____

_____

_____

_____

2. **Decide** Were there any other types of graphs you could have

made using the data? Explain. _____

_____

_____

_____

Connect It

Look at the sales information in the report above. Write a report to show sales information for Marie's Music Store for May, June, July, and August. Then make a graph to show the information you used in your report.

Teacher Notes

Connect: Graphing a Report

Objective Gather information from a report to construct graphs.

Using the Connect (Activities to use after Lesson 5)
This activity requires students to carefully read a report and use the information given to construct various graphs. Students will learn to distinguish between line graphs, bar graphs, and circle graphs. They will be given the opportunity to determine the appropriate graph to use to display different data. The critical thinking questions encourage students to describe how they made their graphs. They also prompt them to think about how different graphs can be used. The Connect It asks students to create their own report and their own graphs.

Math Journal You may wish to have students use their *Math Journals* for the Connect It activity.

Going Beyond Give students a new report filled with enough information for them to create three distinct graphs.

Solutions

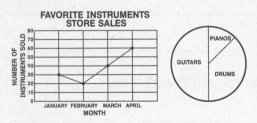

1. *Answers may vary. Sample:* The sales information shows change over time, so I used a line graph. The information about instrument preferences shows parts of a whole, so I used a circle graph.

2. *Answers may vary. Sample:* Yes. I could use a bar graph to show the sales information because bar graphs can be used to compare sales for each month.

Connect It *Answers may vary. Sample:* Sales were not good in May. We only sold 20 instruments. Then in June, we sold 50 instruments. July was our best month ever! We sold 70 instruments. In August, we sold half as many instruments as we sold in May.

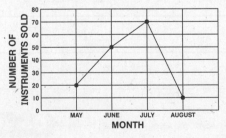

Name _____   Date _____

CHAPTER 16
Explore

Lines and Strings

You can tie pieces of string onto a board to make geometric figures. If you tied a piece of string from peg A to peg E, you would label it $\overline{AE}$.

Think of the pieces of string as line segments. Think of the pegs as points.

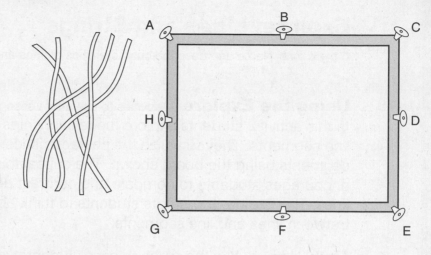

Use the board above to solve the exercises.

1. Find as many ways as you can to tie on pieces of string that are parallel to each other. Write your answers using symbols.

   _____

2. Find as many ways as you can to tie strings to form perpendicular line segments? Write your answers using symbols.

   _____

3. How many ways can you make intersecting line segments by crossing a piece of string with a string tied from peg C to peg G. Write your answers using symbols.

   _____

4. **Compare and Contrast** Compare perpendicular lines to intersecting

   lines. How are the lines alike? How are they different? _____

   _____

Explore It

Explain why the pieces of string on the board are line segments and not lines.

Teacher Notes

Explore: Lines and Strings

Objective Name and describe characteristics of lines and line segments.

Using the Explore (Activities to use after Lesson 1)
In this activity, students explore the relationships between lines and line segments. They visualize the characteristics of lines and line segments using the board shown. The critical thinking question encourages students to compare and contrast different properties of lines. The Explore It prompts students to think about the differences between lines and line segments.

Math Journal You may wish to have students use their *Math Journals* to answer the Explore It question.

Going Beyond Discuss with students lines and line segments in the real world. Explain to them that because lines go on without end, there are no actual lines in the real world, only line segments.

Solutions

1. *Answers may vary. Sample:*
   $\overline{AG} \parallel \overline{BF}$, $\overline{BF} \parallel \overline{CE}$, $\overline{AC} \parallel \overline{HD}$, $\overline{DH} \parallel \overline{EG}$, $\overline{HF} \parallel \overline{AE}$, $\overline{AE} \parallel \overline{BD}$, $\overline{HF} \parallel \overline{BD}$, $\overline{AC} \parallel \overline{GE}$, $\overline{AG} \parallel \overline{CE}$

2. *Answers may vary: Sample:*
   $\overline{AE} \perp \overline{CG}$; $\overline{BF} \perp \overline{HD}$; $\overline{AE} \perp \overline{BH}$; $\overline{AE} \perp \overline{DF}$; $\overline{CG} \perp \overline{BD}$; $\overline{CG} \perp \overline{FH}$

3. 9 ways; $\overline{AD}$, $\overline{AE}$, $\overline{AF}$, $\overline{BD}$, $\overline{BF}$, $\overline{DH}$, $\overline{BE}$, $\overline{HE}$, $\overline{HF}$

4. *Answers may vary. Sample:* Both intersecting and perpendicular lines are lines that cross each other. Perpendicular lines cross each other to form right angles.

Explore It *Answers may vary. Sample:* The pieces of string have endpoints on the board. Lines do not have endpoints.

Name _____ Date _____

Circles and Compasses

A compass is used to help find direction.
It has direction points: N (North), E (East),
S (South), and W (West). The compass is
marked every 10° from 0° to 360°.

Sasha drew this map of her neighborhood
and a compass to show the location of some
of her friends' houses.

**Use the map and the compass to answer
the exercises. You must start at 0° and
move only in the direction of the arrow.**

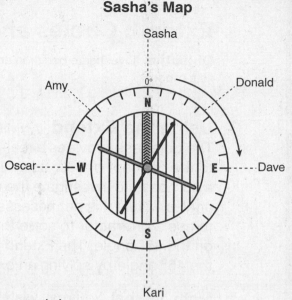

Sasha's Map

1. How many degrees does Sasha have to travel around the

   compass to reach: Dave's house? _____   Kari's house? _____

2. Donald's house is halfway between Sasha's house and Dave's house.

   How many degrees does Sasha travel to reach Donald's house? _____

3. How many more degrees would she need to travel to reach

   Dave's house from Donald's house? _____

4. **Infer** How many 45° angles are there between Sasha's house and

   Kari's house? _____

5. If Sasha traveled $\frac{3}{4}$ of the way around the compass, she would

   stop at which direction point? _____

   How many degrees from North would she have traveled? _____

Extend It

How many degrees does Sasha have to travel around the compass
to reach Amy's house? Explain how you found your answer.

Teacher Notes

Extend: Circles and Compasses

Objective Investigate common angle measures in a circle using a compass as a model.

Using the Extend (Activities to use after Lesson 3)

The compass provides a real-life example that introduces students to the concept of 360° as a full circle. In this activity students use a compass to investigate the relationships between the common angles. While it is not necessary for this activity, students may wish to use a protractor to solve the exercises. Special emphasis is placed on the 45° angle. The Extend It furthers students' understanding of the 45° angle by solving an exercise and explaining their answer.

Math Journal You may wish to have students use their *Math Journals* to answer the Going Beyond.

Going Beyond Ask students to create their own map with a compass similar to the one pictured for this activity. Have them make up problems using their map and compass.

Solutions

1. Dave 90°; Kari 180°

2. 45°

3. 45°

4. 4

5. West; 270°

Extend It 315°; *Answers may vary. Sample:* I know that Oscar's house is at 270°. Amy's house is halfway between Oscar's house and Sasha's house, so I know there are 45° between Oscar's house and Amy's house. 270° + 45° = 315°.

Shapes of States

The outlines of states often look like quadrilaterals or other polygons. This is a simplified map of the United States west of the Mississippi River.

WASHINGTON

OREGON

MONTANA

NORTH DAKOTA

MINNESOTA

IDAHO

SOUTH DAKOTA

WYOMING

NEVADA

NEBRASKA

IOWA

UTAH

COLORADO

CALIFORNIA

KANSAS

MISSOURI

ARIZONA

OKLAHOMA

ARKANSAS

NEW MEXICO

TEXAS

LOUISIANA

N
W ←——○——→ E
S

Use the map to answer the questions.

1. Which state looks the most like a square? _____

2. Which states look most like rectangles? _____

3. Which states look most like hexagons? _____

4. Which state looks the most like a polygon with 7 sides? _____

5. Analyze Which two states look the most like pentagons?

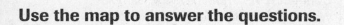

Name two states that are next to each other that together look

like a pentagon. _____

Connect It

Write the states that you think do not look like polygons.
Then explain why you think they do not look like polygons.

Teacher Notes

Connect: Shapes of States

Objective Identify states that resemble geometric figures.

Using the Connect (Activities to use after Lesson 5)
Students enjoy learning from maps. In this activity students are asked to find shapes using a schematic map of the Western United States. This provides an opportunity to apply reasoning skills to answer questions about the shapes of states. The Connect It shows students that not all states will resemble a simple geometric shape.

Math Journal You may wish to have students use their *Math Journals* to answer the Connect It question.

Going Beyond Have students write their own problems about the shapes of states using the map. Make sure students provide answers for their problems.

Solutions

Answers may vary. Samples:

1. Wyoming.

2. Colorado and North Dakota.

3. Iowa and Utah.

4. Texas.

5. Idaho and Nevada; Missouri and Arkansas.

Connect It *Answers may vary. Sample:* Washington and Louisiana do not look like polygons. These states have too many inlets to imagine straight lines.

Congruent Triangles

You can use a ruler to draw lines to divide an equilateral triangle into more than one congruent triangle.

1. Use a ruler to divide this equilateral triangle into 2 congruent triangles. Describe how you divided the triangle.

   _____

   _____

2. Use a ruler to divide this equilateral triangle into 3 congruent triangles. Describe how you divided the triangle.

   _____

   _____

3. Use a ruler to divide this equilateral triangle into 4 congruent triangles. Describe how you divided the triangle.

   _____

   _____

4. How could you use your description for problem 3 to help you divide an equilateral triangle into 8 congruent triangles?

   _____

   _____

Explore It

Describe how you could divide an equilateral triangle into 12 congruent triangles.

Teacher Notes

Explore: Congruent Triangles

Objective Explore how to divide a large equilateral triangle into smaller congruent triangles.
Materials ruler

Using the Explore (Activities to use after Lesson 1)

In this activity, students will further their understanding of congruence by seeing how to divide a large equilateral triangle into smaller triangles that are congruent. Students should be encouraged to notice patterns in how these congruent figures are created. The Explore It asks students to use what they have learned to divide an equilateral triangle into 12 congruent triangles.

Math Journal You may wish to have students use their *Math Journals* to answer the Explore It question.

Going Beyond Have students try to divide an isosceles triangle into multiple congruent triangles.

Solutions

1.

Answers may vary. I drew a line from one vertex to the midpoint of the opposite side.

2.

Answers may vary. I drew lines from each vertex toward the midpoint of the opposite side. Each of the line segments ends at the point where they all meet in the middle of the large triangle.

3.

Answers may vary. I drew a line from the midpoint of each side to the midpoint of the adjacent sides.

4. *Answers may vary.* I know how to divide the triangle into 4 congruent triangles so I could just divide each of those 4 triangles in half.

Explore It *Answers may vary.* I could divide the triangle into 4 congruent triangles and then divide each of those triangles into 3 congruent triangles.

Glide Reflections

A glide reflection is a transformation made by moving a figure with a translation and a reflection. Here are some examples of glide reflections.

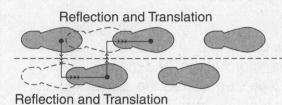

Reflection and Translation

Reflection and Translation

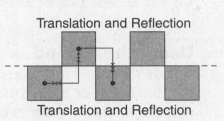

Translation and Reflection

Translation and Reflection

Footprints are a great example of glide reflections. There is a translation and then a reflection.

Glide reflections are used to make patterns. Many of these patterns are used in wallpaper designs.

1. Predict Think of another real world example where glide reflections are used.

_____

**Explain how each of the glide reflections below was created.
Draw arrows to help explain your answer.**

2.

_____
_____

3.

_____
_____

4. Analyze Look at the glide reflections of the squares at the top of this page. Explain how to make this pattern using other transformations.

_____

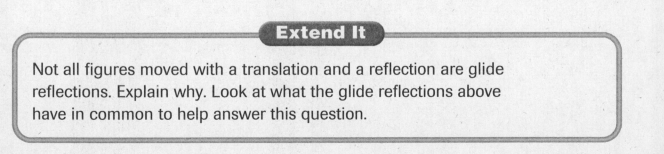

Extend It

Not all figures moved with a translation and a reflection are glide reflections. Explain why. Look at what the glide reflections above have in common to help answer this question.

Teacher Notes

Extend: Glide Reflections

Objective Introduce the properties and uses of glide reflections.

Using the Extend (Activities to use after Lesson 3)

A glide reflection is a type of symmetry transformation. This means that the figure or figures must be reflected and translated the same way each time in order to create a symmetrical pattern. The figure being reflected must also be symmetrical. Students are asked to think of real-world applications of glide reflections. They are also asked how to create patterns using transformations they already know. The Extend It helps students understand the properties of glide reflections and serves as an introduction to the concept of symmetry.

Math Journal You may wish to have students use their *Math Journals* for the Extend It activity.

Going Beyond Have students draw their own glide reflections. Then have students explain why the figures they made are examples of glide reflections.

Solutions

1. *Answers may vary.* Patterns in clothes can be made using glide reflections. Artists can use glide reflections when painting or drawing.

2. *Answers may vary.* The rectangle is reflected over the line and then is moved to the right using a translation.

3. *Answers may vary.* The footprint is moved to the right using a translation and then is reflected over the line.

4. *Answers may vary.* You can move the squares diagonally using translations. You can rotate the square 180 degrees around a point.

Extend It The figures in glide reflections have to be reflected and translated the same way every time to make the patterns. The figure being reflected also has to have symmetry. That way it will look the same when you reflect it.

Symmetry and Letters

Several capital letters in the alphabet have symmetry.
You can draw capital letters to solve the following riddles.

1. I have 1 vertical line of symmetry.
I come after the letter that has 4 lines of symmetry.
What letter am I?   _____

2. I have only 1 line of symmetry.
My line of symmetry is vertical.
I come before a vowel.
What letter am I?   _____

3. I am a vowel.
I have only 1 line of symmetry.
My line of symmetry is horizontal.
What letter am I?   _____

4. I have no lines of symmetry.
The letter after me has 2 lines of symmetry.
You can rotate this letter 90 degrees to
make it become an I.
What letter am I?   _____

5. There are 4 letters in a row that have
no lines of symmetry.
I am the third letter in that group.
What letter am I?   _____

Now unscramble the letters. They spell a branch of mathematics.
Write the word you unscrambled in the spaces below.

____   ____   O   M   E   ____   ____   ____

Connect It

Write your first name using capital letters. Then create your own
riddles for each letter in your name. Your riddles should include
clues about the symmetry of the letters that spell your name.

Teacher Notes

Connect: Symmetry and Letters

Objective Solve riddles that involve some geometric properties (symmetry, rotations, and reflections) of letters.

Using the Connect (Activities to use after Lesson 5)
In this activity, students look at the capital letters and analyze their geometric properties. These include lines of symmetry, as well as what letters look like after using rotations and reflections. The Connect It gives students an opportunity to create riddles using the letters in their own names.

Math Journal You may wish to have students use their *Math Journals* for the Connect It activity.

Going Beyond Have students find an object in the classroom. Ask them to create riddles for the letters in that object's name. When they are finished, have the students exchange riddles. Students should solve the riddles and then see if they can name the object.

Solutions

1. Y

2. T

3. E

4. G

5. R

GEOMETRY

Connect It *Answers may vary. Check students' riddles.*

Name _____   Date _____

Perimeter and Area

Each of the small boxes that make up Figures A through E
is a square. Each of the squares has an area of 1 square unit.

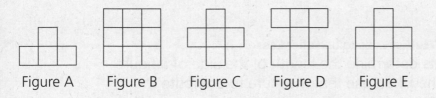

Figure A   Figure B   Figure C   Figure D   Figure E

1. Find the area and perimeter of Figures B through E.
   Fill in the table below. Figure A has been done for you.

Figure	A	B	C	D	E
Perimeter (in units)	10				
Area (in square units)	4				

2. **Analyze** Look at the perimeter and area you found for each of the
   figures. Order the figures from greatest perimeter to least perimeter.
   Then order the figures from greatest area to least area. What do
   you notice about the relationship between the area and perimeter
   of a figure?

   _____

   _____

Explore It

These 3 figures have the same area.

What is the perimeter of each of
these figures?

Figure F   Figure G   Figure H

Figure F _____   Figure G _____   Figure H _____

Describe the relationship between the perimeter and the shape
of these figures.

Teacher Notes

Explore: Perimeter and Area

Objective Compare perimeter and area.

Using the Explore (Activities to use after Lesson 1)
In this activity, students determine the length of the side of a figure given its perimeter. They then use that measure to compute the perimeter and area of other figures. The critical thinking question encourages students to look beyond simply computing perimeter and area. Students are asked to compare the perimeter with the area of figures. The Explore It asks students to apply their understanding to a new situation and describe the relationship(s) they find.

Math Journal You may wish to have students use their *Math Journals* to answer the Explore It.

Going Beyond You can extend the principles learned in this lesson to geography. Encourage students to examine the shapes of states, particularly coastal states and states whose borders are formed by rivers, to realize how much the irregular shapes contribute to the actual length of coastlines or borders.

Solutions

1.

Figure	A	B	C	D	E
Perimeter (in units)	10	12	12	16	14
Area (in square units)	4	9	5	7	6

2. Perimeter from greatest to least: Figure D, Figure E, Figures B and C have the same perimeter, Figure A.

Area from greatest to least: Figure B, Figure D, Figure E, Figure C, Figure A.

Answers may vary. Sample: The figure with the greatest area does not necessarily have the greatest perimeter.

Explore It Figure F: 14 units; Figure G: 12 units; Figure H: 10 units.

Answers may vary. Sample: The perimeter decreases as the shape of the figure more closely resembles a rectangle.

Mowing Lawn Areas

Emily and Greg mow lawns and do yard work
to earn extra money during the summer.

Their neighbor's lawn is shaped like a rectangle.
It is 50 feet long and 40 feet wide. The lawn mower
cuts strips that are 2 feet wide. Greg decides that
he will mow the lawn starting from the outside
edge, and continue around the outside of the yard.
Then, when he reaches the place where he started,
he will continue mowing the outside-uncut edge,
mowing until he has completed half of the lawn.
When half of the lawn has been mowed, Emily
will finish mowing the lawn.

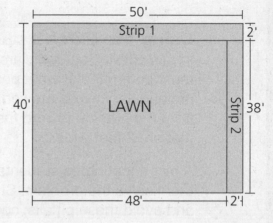

1. Describe how much of the yard Greg mows before Emily takes over.

_____

_____

2. What are the areas of each rectangle he mows? _____

_____

3. How much of a rectangle or side does he finish before turning
   over the mower to Emily? Hint: Use graph paper to draw a picture.
   Be careful at the corners.

_____

Extend It

If Greg and Emily walk 2 feet with every step they take, how many
steps did they both take to mow the lawn? Explain your answer.

Teacher Notes

Extend: Mowing Lawn Areas

Objective Solve real-world problems by computing perimeter and area.

Using the Extend (Activities to use after Lesson 3)

In this activity, students are presented with a problem in which they must determine at what point one-half the area of a 50 foot by 40 foot rectangular lawn is mowed. The lawn is mowed in a given pattern, from the outside toward the center, with a mower that makes cuts that are 2 feet wide.

A hint encourages students to draw a diagram of the pattern to help them solve the problem. Students must carefully analyze the pattern and avoid these pitfalls: counting corners twice, incorrectly determining the length of each section, and computing areas incorrectly.

The Extend It involves finding distance, given the fact that 2 feet is equal to 1 step.

Math Journal You may wish to have students use their *Math Journals* to answer the Extend It question and for their diagram and computations.

Going Beyond Have students design, draw, and label a diagram of an irregularly shaped lawn. Have them make up problems like the one presented in this activity about mowing or using a spreader to seed and fertilize their lawn.

Solutions

1. *Answers may vary. Sample:* Since the lawn is 50 feet long by 40 feet wide, the area of the lawn is 2,000 square feet. Emily will take over when Greg has mowed half, or 1,000 square feet of the lawn.

2. If the mowers start with the long side, the areas of the cuts (in square feet) are 100 + 76 + 96 + 72 + 92 + 68 + 88 + 64 + 84 + 60 + 80 + 56 + 64.

3. If Greg's first cut is along the 50-foot length of the lawn, he completes half the area when he cuts 64 square feet of the 76 square feet cut, along the length.

Extend It *Answers may vary. Sample:* The first cut requires 25 steps. The second cut requires 19 steps. The total number of steps is 25 + 19 + 24 + 18 + 23 + 17 + . . . + 6 + 1. The total number of steps is 500.

Each strip requires one-fourth the number of steps as its area. So, the total number of steps is one-fourth the total area, which is 2,000 square feet. So, the total number of steps is 500.

More Prisms

Look at the nets below. A net for a triangular prism is shown on the left.
A net for a rectangular prism with square bases is shown on the right.

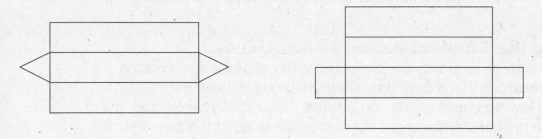

1. Draw a net for a pentagonal prism and a net for a hexagonal prism.
   Draw the bases as regular polygons.

   Pentagonal Prism Net   Hexagonal Prism Net

2. What is the relationship between the number of faces
   and the number of sides of the base?

   _____

3. A 12-inch long rectangular prism has square bases with sides
   that are each 4 inches. The surface area of a prism is the sum
   of the areas of all the faces including the bases. What is the
   surface area of this rectangular prism?

   _____

Connect It

Write a formula that you can use to find the surface area of
a rectangular prism having a base L units long and W units
wide, with a height of H units.

Teacher Notes

Connect: More Prisms

Objective Identify prisms from faces and bases and explore surface area.

Using the Connect (Activities to use after Lesson 5)

In this activity, students are presented with nets for prisms having bases with 3 and 4 sides. They are then asked to draw nets for prisms having bases with 5 and 6 sides. This activity helps students see the relationship between the number of sides of the base and the number of rectangular faces. The activity also explores the concept of surface area. The Connect It encourages students to extend their understanding of surface area by asking them to write a formula for finding surface area that reflects the method they used to find the surface area of the rectangular prism in Problem 3.

Math Journal You may wish to have students use their *Math Journals* to draw the nets and for the Connect It activity.

Going Beyond Ask students to develop a method for finding the surface area of a triangular prism. They will need to find the area of the triangle bases.

Solutions

1. *Answers may vary. Sample:*

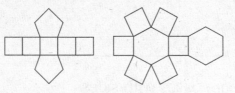

2. The number of faces is equal to the number of sides of the base.

3. The area of each of the prism's two square bases is 16 square inches.

The area of each of the prism's four rectangular faces is 48 square inches. The surface area of the rectangular prism is 16 + 16 + 48 + 48 + 48 + 48 = 224 square inches. This can also be written as 2(16) square inches + 4(48) square inches = 224 square inches.

Connect It *Answers may vary. Sample:* $SA = 2LW + 4WH$

Fractions Between Fractions

You can use number lines to find fractions between fractions. Look at the number lines at right. The dotted lines between the number lines show fractions that are equivalent.

1. Use the number lines at right to find a fraction between $\frac{1}{3}$ and $\frac{2}{3}$.

Use the number lines at right to answer Exercises 2–3.

2. Find a fraction between $\frac{1}{4}$ and $\frac{2}{4}$.

_____

3. Use the sixteenths number line to find another fraction between $\frac{1}{4}$ and $\frac{2}{4}$.

_____

Use the number lines at right to answer Exercise 4.

4. Find a fraction between $\frac{2}{5}$ and $\frac{4}{5}$. Explain how you know that the fraction is between $\frac{2}{5}$ and $\frac{4}{5}$.

_____

_____

_____

Explore It

Draw a number line showing twentieths under the number lines in Exercise 4. Explain how this number line helps you find other fractions between $\frac{2}{5}$ and $\frac{4}{5}$.

Teacher Notes

Explore: Fractions Between Fractions

Objective Use number lines to find fractions between fractions.

Using the Explore (Activities to use after Lesson 2)

In this activity, students use number lines that show equivalent fractions to find fractions between other fractions. The Explore It asks students to create another number line to find more equivalent fractions.

Math Journal You may wish to have students use their *Math Journals* to answer the Explore It question.

Going Beyond Have students research the density property. Highly motivated students may find it exciting to use an algebra book as a resource. This property states that between any pair of rational numbers, there is another rational number. Ask students how they think this property affects the number of fractions between fractions.

Solutions

1. *Answers may vary. Sample:* $\frac{5}{12}$
2. *Answers may vary. Sample:* $\frac{3}{8}$
3. *Answers may vary. Sample:* $\frac{5}{16}$
4. *Answers may vary. Sample:* $\frac{5}{10}$, $\frac{6}{10}$, or $\frac{7}{10}$. The dotted lines connect equivalent fractions, so any fraction between the dotted lines for $\frac{2}{5}$ and $\frac{4}{5}$ is between $\frac{2}{5}$ and $\frac{4}{5}$.

Explore It *Number lines may vary. Sample:*

Answers may vary. Sample: The twentieths number line shows 4 fractions between the dotted lines for $\frac{2}{5}$ and $\frac{4}{5}$.

Name _____   Date _____

CHAPTER 19
Extend

Cross Products

You can use multiplication to check if two fractions are equivalent.

You can multiply the numerator and the denominator by the same number.

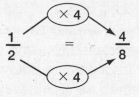

The numerator and the denominator of $\frac{1}{2}$ are both multiplied by 4, so $\frac{1}{2} = \frac{4}{8}$.

You can also cross multiply to find cross products.

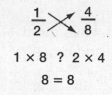

$$1 \times 8 \ ? \ 2 \times 4$$
$$8 = 8$$

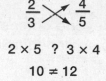

$$2 \times 5 \ ? \ 3 \times 4$$
$$10 \neq 12$$

The cross products are equal, so the fractions are equivalent.

The cross products are not equal, so the fractions are not equivalent.

Try these on your own. Write = or ≠. You can use a calculator for Exercises 7 through 9.

1. $\frac{4}{5} \bigcirc \frac{12}{15}$

2. $\frac{3}{4} \bigcirc \frac{6}{8}$

3. $\frac{1}{10} \bigcirc \frac{10}{1,000}$

4. $\frac{3}{8} \bigcirc \frac{4}{9}$

5. $\frac{7}{9} \bigcirc \frac{8}{11}$

6. $\frac{4}{25} \bigcirc \frac{8}{50}$

7. $\frac{15}{21} \bigcirc \frac{63}{90}$

8. $\frac{32}{83} \bigcirc \frac{128}{332}$

9. $\frac{14}{42} \bigcirc \frac{121}{363}$

10. **Hypothesize** Do you think you can use cross products to compare fractions that are not equivalent? How can you tell which fraction is greater? Give an example.

Extend It

Use cross products to find the value of x in $\frac{x}{12} = \frac{6}{8}$.

Houghton Mifflin Math • Chapter Challenges   **111**

Teacher Notes

Extend: Cross Products

Objective Use cross products to identify equivalent fractions.

Using the Extend (Activities to use after Lesson 3)
In this activity, students are introduced to using cross products as another way of determining if fractions are equivalent. The critical thinking question asks students to think of a way to use cross products to compare fractions that are not equivalent. For the Extend It, students use cross products to solve an equation with a variable.

Math Journal You may wish to have students use their *Math Journals* for the Extend It problem.

Going Beyond After students complete the Extend It, have them make up similar equations and solve, using a variable and cross products.

Solutions

1. $=$
2. $=$
3. $\neq$
4. $\neq$
5. $\neq$
6. $=$
7. $\neq$
8. $=$
9. $=$

10. *Answers may vary. Sample:* Yes. For example, you know that $\frac{1}{2} > \frac{1}{4}$. Cross multiply and compare the products: $4 > 2$. You know that the unit fraction with the greater denominator is the lesser fraction. So, $\frac{1}{2} > \frac{1}{4}$.

Extend It *Answers may vary. Sample:* First find cross products: $8x = 72$. Then divide both sides by 8. Solution: $x = 9$

Name _____ Date _____

Simplify in One Step

You can simplify fractions using the greatest common denominator, or GCF.

Factor the numerator and denominator using prime numbers. Circle pairs of numbers that appear in both prime factorizations.

2 and 3 appear in both prime factorizations.

$$2 \times 3 = 6$$

Divide the numerator and denominator by the GCF.

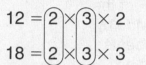

The GCF of 12 and 18 is 6.

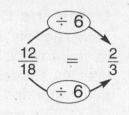

To help endangered animals, people make plans for the animals' recovery. The chart on this page shows the names of some endangered or threatened groups of species. The fractions in the chart show what part of each group listed has a recovery plan.

Look at the data in the chart. Use the GCF to simplify the fractions in Exercises 1–6 in the chart.

	Group	Fraction with Recovery Plan	Fraction in Simplest Form
1.	Crustaceans	$\frac{12}{21}$	
2.	Amphibians	$\frac{12}{27}$	
3.	Insects	$\frac{28}{46}$	
4.	Reptiles	$\frac{30}{115}$	
5.	Fishes	$\frac{95}{125}$	
6.	Mammals	$\frac{50}{340}$	

Connect It

How is finding the GCF in problem 6 different from finding the GCF in problems 1–5?

Teacher Notes

Connect: Simplify in One Step

Objective Use the GCF to simplify fractions.

Using the Connect (Activities to use after Lesson 5)

In this activity, students are presented with data in fraction form related to recovery plans for endangered and threatened animal species. Students use prime factorization to find the GCF of the numerator and denominator of each fraction and then divide by the GCF to simplify in one step. The Connect It gives students more experience with fractions in which two factors must be multiplied to get the GCF.

Math Journal You may wish to have students use their *Math Journals* for the Connect It activity.

Going Beyond Have students research to find fractions of plant species groups that have plans for recovery. Then have students present their results.

Solutions

1. $12 = 2 \times 2 \times 3$
   $21 = 3 \times 7$
   GCF: 3
   Simplest form: $\frac{4}{7}$

2. $12 = 2 \times 2 \times 3$
   $27 = 3 \times 3 \times 3$
   GCF: 3
   Simplest form: $\frac{4}{9}$

3. $28 = 2 \times 2 \times 7$
   $46 = 2 \times 23$
   GCF: 2
   Simplest form: $\frac{14}{23}$

4. $30 = 2 \times 3 \times 5$
   $115 = 5 \times 23$
   GCF: 5
   Simplest form: $\frac{6}{23}$

5. $95 = 5 \times 19$
   $125 = 5 \times 5 \times 5$
   GCF: 5
   Simplest form: $\frac{19}{25}$

6. $50 = 2 \times 5 \times 5$
   $340 = 2 \times 2 \times 5 \times 17$
   GCF: $2 \times 5 = 10$
   Simplest form: $\frac{5}{34}$

Connect It *Answers may vary. Sample:* You have to multiply two factors to get the GCF in problem 6.

Fraction Patterns

In this triangle, the number in each circle is equal to the sum of the fractions in the two circles above it.

Fill in the circles to complete the triangle. Then find the sum of the fractions in each row.

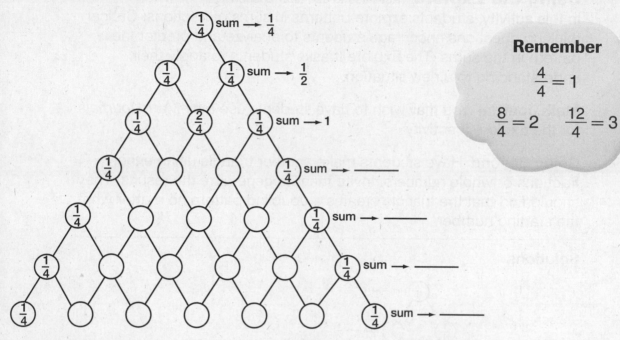

Remember

$$\frac{4}{4} = 1$$

$$\frac{8}{4} = 2 \qquad \frac{12}{4} = 3$$

1. **Analyze** What pattern do you see in the sums of the fractions

   in each row? _____

   _____

2. **Predict** What is the sum for the next row of fractions? _____

   Extend the pattern of fractions by 1 row and add to verify your

   prediction. _____

Explore It

On a separate sheet of paper, make a triangle pattern with 8 rows like the one on this page. Use $\frac{1}{2}$ in the circle at the top of your triangle. What do you notice in the pattern of the sums?

Teacher Notes

Explore: Fraction Patterns

Objective Find patterns in sums of fractions.

Using the Explore (Activities to use after Lesson 1)

In this activity, students explore patterns in sums of fractions. Critical thinking questions encourage students to analyze and predict the pattern in the sums. The Explore It asks students to apply their understanding to a new situation.

Math Journal You may wish to have students use their *Math Journals* for the Explore It activity.

Going Beyond Have students make another triangle using either fractions or whole numbers. Invite them to generalize the results. They should find that the triangle creates a doubling pattern no matter what the starting number.

Solutions

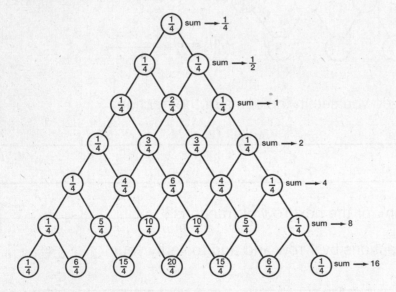

1. The sums double each time.

2. 32; $\frac{1}{4}, \frac{7}{4}, \frac{21}{4}, \frac{35}{4}, \frac{35}{4}, \frac{21}{4}, \frac{7}{4}, \frac{1}{4}$

Explore It *Answers may vary. Check students' triangles.* The sums double.

Fraction Sums

There is more than one way to add fractions with unlike denominators.
Here is a method that uses multiplication and addition.

$$\frac{3}{4} + \frac{1}{6} = \frac{(3 \times 6) + (4 \times 1)}{4 \times 6} = \frac{\square + 4}{\square} = \frac{\square}{\square}$$

1. Write the fraction in simplest form. _____

2. **Explain** Describe the method of adding fractions with unlike denominators.

   _____

   _____

   _____

Use the method to find these sums. Write your answer in simplest form.

3. $\frac{1}{2} + \frac{1}{8} =$ _____

4. $\frac{1}{3} + \frac{1}{4} =$ _____

5. $\frac{3}{5} + \frac{2}{3} =$ _____

6. $\frac{5}{6} + \frac{1}{3} =$ _____

7. $\frac{1}{5} + \frac{1}{4} =$ _____

8. $\frac{2}{7} + \frac{1}{2} =$ _____

9. $\frac{2}{5} + \frac{2}{3} =$ _____

10. $\frac{2}{9} + \frac{3}{5} =$ _____

11. $\frac{5}{8} + \frac{4}{6} =$ _____

12. **Generalize** Using variables for the fractions, $\frac{a}{b}$ and $\frac{c}{d}$, write a formula that shows this method for finding the sum of fractions with unlike denominators.

   _____

Extend It

On a separate sheet of paper, describe another method to add fractions with unlike denominators.

Teacher Notes

Extend: Fraction Sums

Objective Find sums of fractions with unlike denominators.

Using the Extend (Activities to use after Lesson 6)
The usual way to add fractions with unlike denominators is to find equivalent fractions with a common denominator, and then find the sums of the numerators. In this activity, students learn another way to add fractions that will carry over to algebra. Critical thinking questions encourage students to describe and analyze the algorithm. The Extend It asks students to develop another method of finding the sum of fractions with unlike denominators.

Math Journal You may wish to have students use their *Math Journals* for the Extend It activity.

Going Beyond Have students write a word problem in which they predict the results of the difference between two fractions with unlike denominators. For example, Greg lives $\frac{5}{8}$ of a mile from the library. Emily lives $\frac{1}{4}$ of a mile from the library. Does Greg live more than $\frac{1}{2}$ mile farther from the library than Emily? Students should see that for the difference to be $\frac{1}{2}$ mile, then Greg would have to live $\frac{3}{4}$ mile or Emily would have to live $\frac{1}{8}$ mile from the library. Since $\frac{5}{8}$ is less than $\frac{3}{4}$ or $\frac{1}{4}$ is greater than $\frac{1}{8}$, students should predict that the difference is less than $\frac{1}{2}$ mile.

Solutions

$$\frac{3}{4} + \frac{1}{6} = \frac{(3 \times 6) + (4 \times 1)}{4 \times 6} = \frac{18 + 4}{24} = \frac{22}{24}$$

1. Simplest form: $\frac{11}{12}$

2. *Answers may vary. Sample:* Multiply the numerator of the first fraction by the denominator of the second fraction, and the denominator of the first fraction by the numerator of the second fraction, then add the products. Place that sum over the product of the denominators, and simplify the resulting fraction.

3. $\frac{5}{8}$ **4.** $\frac{7}{12}$ **5.** $1\frac{4}{15}$

6. $1\frac{1}{6}$ **7.** $\frac{9}{20}$ **8.** $\frac{11}{14}$

9. $1\frac{1}{15}$ **10.** $\frac{37}{45}$ **11.** $1\frac{7}{24}$

12. $\frac{a}{b} + \frac{c}{d} = \frac{(a \times d) + (b \times c)}{b \times d}$

Extend It *Answers may vary. Sample:* Use fraction strips to show both fractions. Then use the strips to write equivalent fractions with a common denominator. Add the numerators and write the fraction in simplest form.

Build a Garden

Aimee is building a rectangular garden. One side has a length of $5\frac{1}{3}$ yards. The perimeter of the garden is $18\frac{2}{3}$ yards.

> The perimeter of a rectangle is the sum of the length of its sides.

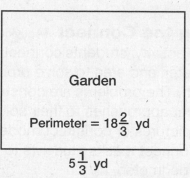

Garden

Perimeter $= 18\frac{2}{3}$ yd

$5\frac{1}{3}$ yd

1. Find the lengths of the missing sides and write them on the rectangle. How did you find the answer?

_____

_____

2. Aimee will use boards made of recycled plastic lumber to build the border around the garden. The boards are sold in lengths of 10 feet, 12 feet, 14 feet, and 16 feet. Which length of boards should she buy so that she uses the least amount of lumber?

> 1 yd = 3 ft

_____

3. **Predict** Aimee is planting broccoli in her garden. Each broccoli plant needs an area of about $1\frac{1}{2}$ square feet. About how many broccoli plants can she put in the garden? Explain.

_____

_____

Connect It

Design a garden with a perimeter of $20\frac{3}{4}$ ft. Your garden may be in the shape of a triangle, square, rectangle, or pentagon.

Teacher Notes

Connect: Build a Garden

Objective Solve multi-step problems using fractions, perimeter, and area.

Using the Connect (Activities to use after Lesson 6)

In this activity, students connect their understanding of fractions, perimeter, and area to solve problems related to building a rectangular garden. The problems are constructed so that students can take different approaches to their solutions. Students may find it helpful to draw pictures or construct models to help them solve the problems. The Connect It asks students to design their own garden with a given perimeter.

Math Journal You may wish to have students record their garden designs for the Connect It in their *Math Journals*.

Going Beyond Have students research how much space various fruits or vegetables need to grow. Ask them to design a garden that will fit several of their favorite plants.

Solutions

1.

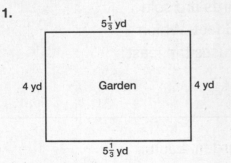

Answers may vary. Sample: Since this is a rectangle, opposite sides have the same length. I know that two sides have a length of $5\frac{1}{3}$ yards. Subtract the sum of these sides from the perimeter: $18\frac{2}{3} - 10\frac{2}{3} = 8$ yards. Each of the remaining sides is half of 8 yards, so the other two lengths are each 4 yards.

2. *Answers may vary. Sample:* Aimee should buy two 12-ft boards and two 16-ft boards; 4 yd = 12 ft and $5\frac{1}{3}$ yd = 16 ft.

3. *Answers may vary. Sample:* About 80 broccoli plants; she can fit about 4 plants per square yard and she has about 5 yd × 4 yd of space: $4 \times 5 \times 4 = 80$

Connect It *Answers may vary. Sample:*

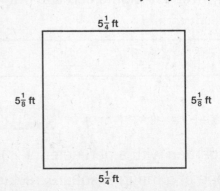

Fraction and Decimal Models

Here are two ways to model the fraction $\frac{5}{10}$.

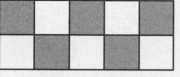

1. Show two more ways to model $\frac{5}{10}$ on these grids.

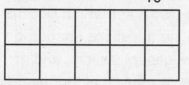

2. What is the decimal equivalent of $\frac{5}{10}$? _____

3. What other ways can you model $\frac{5}{10}$? You can use a grid, or you can use a different way to model $\frac{5}{10}$. Draw one of your ideas below.

4. **Generalize** What is always true about the models for $\frac{5}{10}$? What changes?

_____

5. **Infer** The models above show that $\frac{5}{10}$ is equivalent to 0.5. Can you prove that $\frac{1}{2}$ is equivalent to 0.5? Explain. _____

_____

Explore It

Use grid paper to show at least four different ways to model $\frac{50}{100}$. What is the decimal equivalent of $\frac{50}{100}$?

Teacher Notes

Explore: Fraction and Decimal Models

Objective Model fractions and decimals in a variety of ways.
Materials grid paper

Using the Explore (Activities to use after Lesson 1)

In this activity, students explore different ways the fraction $\frac{5}{10}$ can be modeled. They use these models to discover that the decimal equivalent of $\frac{5}{10}$ is 0.5. The critical thinking questions encourage students to use what they learn to make generalizations and inferences. The Explore It asks students to apply their understanding to a new situation.

Going Beyond Students discovered that $\frac{5}{10}$ and 0.5 are equivalent to $\frac{1}{2}$. Have students find fraction equivalents for 0.75, such as $\frac{75}{100}$ and $\frac{3}{4}$.

Solutions

1. *Answers may vary. Sample:*

   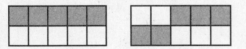

2. 0.5

3. *Answers may vary. Sample:*

4. *Answers may vary. Sample:* The models always show 5 parts out of 10 shaded, or half of the parts shaded. The actual parts that are shaded changes.

5. *Answers may vary. Sample:* Yes. The shaded models show that $\frac{5}{10}$ is equivalent to 0.5. Half of each model is shaded, which proves that $\frac{5}{10}$ is equivalent to $\frac{1}{2}$. So, $\frac{5}{10} = 0.5 = \frac{1}{2}$.

   Explore It $\frac{50}{100} = 0.50$; *Answers may vary. Each model should have 100 equal parts with 50 parts shaded.*

Fraction and Decimal Patterns

Fraction and decimal equivalents can make interesting patterns.
Complete this pattern for fifths.

$\frac{1}{5}$	$\frac{2}{5}$	$\frac{3}{5}$					
0.2	0.4	0.6					

1. Describe the pattern of the decimals for fifths. _____

2. **Predict** Based on the pattern, what decimal is equivalent to $2\frac{1}{5}$? _____

Now complete these tables for halves and fourths.

$\frac{1}{2}$	1	$1\frac{1}{2}$					
0.5	1.0						

$\frac{1}{4}$	$\frac{2}{4}$	$\frac{3}{4}$					
0.25	0.5						

3. What is the pattern of the decimals for halves? _____

What is the pattern of the decimals for fourths? _____

4. **Generalize** How can you use patterns to find equivalent fractions and decimals?

_____

Extend It

Use the table below to create your own pattern using equivalent fractions
and decimals. Then use the pattern to find an equivalent fraction and
decimal not shown in your table.

Teacher Notes

Extend: Fraction and Decimal Patterns

Objective Look for patterns in equivalent fractions and decimals.

Using the Extend (Activities to use after Lesson 4)

Equivalent fractions and decimals express the same amount in different forms. In this activity, students see how the decimal equivalents of common fractions create patterns. The critical thinking questions prompt students to analyze the patterns and make generalizations. The Extend It provides an opportunity for students to create and use their own pattern of fraction and decimal equivalents.

Math Journal You may wish to have students use their *Math Journals* to write the equivalent fractions for the Extend It activity.

Going Beyond Give students exercises with fractions and mixed numbers and have them use patterns to find decimal equivalents.

Solutions

$\frac{1}{5}$	$\frac{2}{5}$	$\frac{3}{5}$	$\frac{4}{5}$	1	$1\frac{1}{5}$	$1\frac{2}{5}$	$1\frac{3}{5}$
0.2	0.4	0.6	0.8	1.0	1.2	1.4	1.6

1. The decimals increase by 0.2.

2. 2.2

$\frac{1}{2}$	1	$1\frac{1}{2}$	2	$2\frac{1}{2}$	3	$3\frac{1}{2}$	4
0.5	1.0	1.5	2.0	2.5	3.0	3.5	4.0

$\frac{1}{4}$	$\frac{2}{4}$	$\frac{3}{4}$	1	$1\frac{1}{4}$	$1\frac{2}{4}$	$1\frac{3}{4}$	2
0.25	0.5	.75	1.00	1.25	1.50	1.75	2.00

3. Halves: the decimals increase by 0.5; fourths: the decimals increase by 0.25.

4. *Answers may vary. Sample:* I can find the pattern in the equivalent fractions and decimals for numbers 0 to 1. Then I can use the pattern to find an equivalent mixed number and decimal for numbers greater than 1.

Extend It *Tables may vary, but should be similar to the tables found on the page. Students should use the table to find an equivalent fraction and decimal that are not shown in their tables.*

Name _____ Date _____

Math Analogies

An analogy is a statement that compares the relationship between
two pairs of objects. The following is an example of a word analogy.
The word "as" separates the two pairs of objects.

Mitten is to hand *as* sock is to foot.

1. What are the pairs of objects? _____

What is the relationship between each pair of objects? _____

_____

Here is a math analogy. It is a statement that compares the
relationship between two pairs of numbers.

$\frac{1}{10}$ is to $\frac{1}{100}$ *as* 0.1 is to 0.01.

2. Analyze What is the relationship between each pair of numbers? _____

_____

**Use your knowledge of fractions and decimals to complete the
math analogies.**

3. $\frac{1}{5}$ is to $\frac{1}{10}$ as 0.2 is to _____.   **4.** $\frac{1}{2}$ is to 0.5 as $\frac{1}{4}$ is to _____.

5. $\frac{4}{12}$ is to $\frac{1}{3}$ as $\frac{3}{12}$ is to _____.   **6.** $5\frac{1}{4}$ is to 5 as 5.25 is to _____.

7. 3.6 is to 0.6 as _____ is to $\frac{3}{5}$.   **8.** 1.7 is to $\frac{17}{10}$ as _____ is to $\frac{17}{100}$.

9. $\frac{3}{100}$ is to $\frac{3}{10}$ as 0.03 is to _____.   **10.** 4 is to $\frac{1}{4}$ as _____ is to $\frac{1}{3}$.

11. $\frac{7}{100}$ is to $\frac{7}{1,000}$ as _____ is to 0.007.   **12.** $\frac{75}{100}$ is to $\frac{50}{100}$ as $\frac{3}{4}$ is to _____.

13. Generalize Explain how to solve an analogy that uses pairs of numbers.

_____

Connect It

Write other math analogies. Use fractions, decimals, or other math concepts.

Teacher Notes

Connect: Math Analogies

Objective Use analogies to analyze how fractions and decimals are related.

Using the Connect (Activities to use after Lesson 5)
Students will frequently see analogies on standardized tests. Solving an analogy requires students to use logical reasoning and their knowledge of the subject. In this activity, students solve fraction, mixed number, and decimal analogies, requiring them to analyze how pairs of these numbers are related. The Connect It activity provides students with an opportunity to create their own math analogies.

Math Journal You may wish to have students use their *Math Journals* to write analogies for the Connect It activity.

Going Beyond Have students prepare a set of analogy cards. Each card should have a math analogy on the front and the answer on the back. Allow them to compete with classmates to solve their analogies.

Solutions

1. mitten, hand; sock, foot. *Answers may vary. Sample:* A mitten covers and protects a hand; a sock covers and protects a foot.

2. *Answers may vary. Sample:* $\frac{1}{10}$ is ten times greater than $\frac{1}{100}$; 0.1 is ten times greater than 0.01.

3. 0.1

4. 0.25

5. $\frac{1}{4}$

6. 5.0

7. $3\frac{3}{5}$

8. 0.17

9. 0.3

10. 3

11. 0.07

12. $\frac{1}{2}$

13. *Answers may vary. Sample:* To solve an analogy, examine the relationship between the first pair of numbers. Then look at the given number in the second pair and decide what number is related to that number in the same way.

Connect It *Answers may vary. Samples:*
25% is to 100% as $\frac{1}{4}$ is to 1;
5 is to 10 as 40 is to 80.

Round Rule

The idea of this decimal game is to identify what makes
a group of decimals similar, or which decimal is different
from the others in the group, based on a rounding rule.

1. **Analyze** Inez says the following decimals: 5.42, 4.6, 4.39, and 5.08.
   Which decimal does not belong in the group? Explain why.

   _____

2. Tory names these decimals: 35.687, 48.569, 85.768, and 52.341.
   Which decimal does not belong in the group? Explain your thinking.

   _____

3. Andrew's decimals are 5.362, 2.15, 4.794, and 6.58. What
   do Andrew's decimals have in common? Name two more
   decimals that could be included on Andrew's list.

   _____

   _____

4. Trisha's decimals are 8.09, 15.2, 7.483, and 37.11. What do
   Trisha's decimals have in common? Name two decimals less
   than 5 that could be included on Trisha's list.

   _____

   _____

5. **Infer** Alison uses the decimals 1.233, 6.201, 2.005, and 0.423.
   Which decimal does not belong in the group? Why?

   _____

   _____

Explore It

Each of the following decimals extends to the ten thousandths place:
2.61<u>3</u>8 and 2.35<u>4</u>2. Round each decimal to the place of the underlined
digit. Explain how you rounded. What is the value of the place underlined?

Teacher Notes

Explore: Round Rule

Objective Use rounding to investigate number patterns involving decimals.

Using the Explore (Activities to use after Lesson 1)

In this activity, students examine a group of decimals and try to identify a similar characteristic based on rounding. They are challenged to think about how each group of decimals is related without knowledge of how they are rounded. In the Explore It students can extend rules for rounding to include rounding to the nearest thousandths. They are introduced to the ten thousandths place so that they can round to the nearest thousandth.

Math Journal You may wish to have students use their *Math Journals* to answer the Explore It activity.

Going Beyond Have students play their own version of the decimal rounding game. Encourage them to develop other rules for the game that do not depend upon rounding. Discuss their rules.

Solutions

1. *Answers may vary. Sample:* 4.39, because it is the only decimal that does not round to 5.

2. *Answers may vary. Sample:* 52.341, because it is the only decimal that does not round up.

3. *Answers may vary. Sample:* They each round up when you round to the nearest tenth. *Sample:* 5.08 and 4.263.

4. *Answers may vary. Sample:* They each round down when you round to the nearest whole number. *Sample:* 3.24 and 2.1.

5. *Answers may vary. Sample:* 2.005, because it is the only decimal that rounds up when rounded to the hundredths place.

Explore It 2.614 and 2.354; *Answers may vary. Sample:* I used the same rules for rounding to other decimal places. The decimals are rounded to the nearest thousandth.

Name _____ Date _____

Time Capsule Map

Students in Mr. Lenox's class made a time capsule. They buried
it and want to make a map so they can dig it up at the end of the
school year. Use the data below to help them make the map.

1. The compass rose shows the
directions north, south, east,
and west as they appear on a
map. Use the compass rose to
help you make the map. The
box represents the playground.
The students start at the
southwest corner of the playground.
Label a starting point, *A*, in the
southwest corner of the playground.

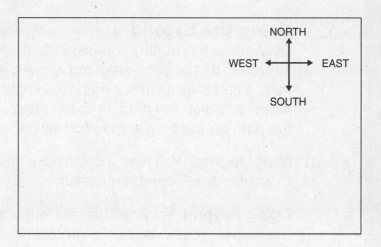

2. Complete the map by drawing lines to show each of these directions.
Then label the length of each direction on your map.

From *A*, walk 3.8 meter north.
Then walk 0.6 meter east, 1.4 meters south,
2.9 meters east, 2.4 meters north, 1.3 meters west,
0.9 meter south, 0.4 meter east, 0.3 meter north,
0.2 meter west, and 0.1 meter south.
Put an *X* to mark this last point to show the location of the time capsule.

3. Analyze How far is it from Point *A* to Point *X*? _____

Extend It

Is this route from Point *A* to Point *X* the shortest route to the
time capsule? Explain your thinking.

Teacher Notes

Extend: Time Capsule Map

Objective Make and use a map.

Using the Extend (Activities to use after Lesson 3)
Students are probably somewhat familiar with reading distances on a map. In this activity, students follow a set of directions to make a map. Then they use their map to compute the total distance they have represented on the map. In Extend It students are asked to decide if the path on the map is the shortest path to the destination.

Math Journal You may wish to have students use their *Math Journals* to answer the Extend It question.

Going Beyond Provide students with road maps. Have them use the maps to compare the lengths of different routes from the same starting point to a given destination. Discuss reasons for a variety of routes.

Solutions

1–2. *Answers may vary. Sample map:*

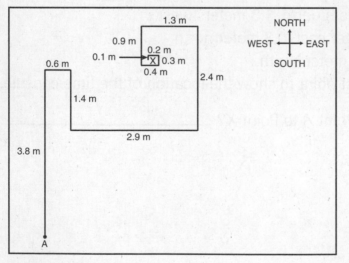

3. 14.3 meters.

Extend It *Answers may vary. Sample:* No. It is not the shortest route. A straight diagonal line from the starting point to the point where *X* marks the time capsule would be the shortest route.

Patterns, Sums, and Differences

Sometimes you can use a sum or a difference to help you
find and extend a pattern. Use each pattern below to solve.
You may use models if you like.

1. Use decimals to describe the pattern in the decimal models.

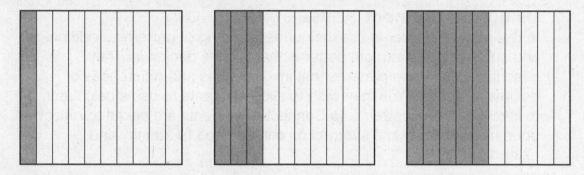

What is the next decimal in the pattern? _____

What is the sum of the first four decimals in the pattern? _____

2. What are the next two decimals in the following pattern:

0.29, 0.26, 0.23, 0.20? _____

What is the difference between the first decimal in the

pattern and the sixth decimal in the pattern? _____

3. Compare and Contrast Find the missing numbers in each pattern.
Then describe how the two patterns are similar and how they are different.

Pattern A: 0.25, _____, 0.75, 1.00, 1.25, _____

Pattern B: 3.00, 2.75, _____, 2.25, 2.00, _____

_____

_____

Connect It

Explain how addition and subtraction can help you describe and
extend a pattern.

Teacher Notes

Connect: Patterns, Sums, and Differences

Objective Use sums and differences to investigate decimal patterns.
Materials calculator (optional)

Using the Connect (Activities to use after Lesson 5)

In this activity, students use their understanding of patterns, addition, and subtraction to explore patterns that involve decimals. They describe and extend patterns that involve sums and differences of decimal numbers. You may wish to allow students to use a calculator to investigate the patterns. In Connect It, students are asked to reflect upon how addition and subtraction can be used to identify and extend patterns.

Math Journal You may wish to have students use their *Math Journals* for the Connect It activity.

Going Beyond Have students explore other patterns using whole numbers or money that involve products using a calculator. Compare these patterns with those that arise using addition. The numbers in patterns that increase by a common product will grow much faster than those that arise from a common sum.

Solutions

1. *Answers may vary. Sample:* The decimals increase by 0.2 each time; 0.7; 1.6.

2. 0.17 and 0.14; 0.15.

3. Pattern A: 0.50 and 1.50; Pattern B: 2.50 and 1.75; *Answers may vary. Sample:* Patterns are similar because they both change by the same amount. They are different because one increases and the other decreases.

Connect It *Answers may vary. Sample:* You can subtract to find how pairs of numbers change in a pattern. Then you can add or subtract the amount to extend the pattern.

Surveys and Samples

People often use surveys to collect data. The part of a population that is surveyed is called a **sample**. The different methods of collecting data are called **sampling techniques**.

1. **Decide** Choose a simple question of interest you could ask your classmates. Then predict the most popular response.

   Question: _____

   Prediction: _____

Write your answers to Exercises 2–5 on a separate sheet of paper.

2. A **random sample** is a group that represents the whole population. Put the names of all your classmates in a paper bag. Mix up the names and draw 5 names out of the bag without looking. Record the names and ask these students your question. Record your results.

3. A **convenience sample** is one in which the subjects chosen are easiest to reach or the sampling is done easily. Ask 5 students who sit around you your question. Record your results.

4. A **systematic sample** is one in which one subject is selected at random and the remaining subjects are selected according to a pattern. Use an alphabetical list of your classmates. Pick one student from the first 5 names on the list. Then select every fourth student on the list. Record the names and ask these students your question. Record your results.

5. **Analyze** Compare the survey results for each sampling method. How do they compare to your prediction?

Explore It

Describe the three sampling techniques you used. Which one do you think is the most fair? Why?

Teacher Notes

Explore: Surveys and Samples

Objective Investigate different sampling techniques.

Using the Explore (Activities to use after Lesson 1)

Students are probably familiar with simple surveys. Statisticians have designed different techniques to choose a sample from a given population. In this activity, students explore three different sampling techniques. They design their own question and make an initial prediction. Then they compare the results they obtain using three different sampling techniques. The Explore It challenges students to summarize their understanding of the different techniques and to choose which one they think is the most representative (free of bias).

Math Journal You may wish to have students use their *Math Journals* to answer Exercises 2–5 and the Explore It question.

Going Beyond Point out that the size of the population used for the students' surveys was very small. Discuss why the results may not reflect preferences of a broader range of students. You may also wish to discuss how to design a fair question.

Solutions

1. *Answers may vary. Sample:* Question: What is your favorite pet? Prediction: dog

2. *Answers may vary. Sample:* José: cat, Elaine: bird, Jill: dog, Luis: dog, Chalice: dog

3. *Answers may vary. Sample:* Manuel: dog, Kim: cat, José: cat, Aman: fish, Omar: dog

4. *Answers may vary. Sample:* Kim: cat, Jill: dog, Joseph: dog, Andrea: cat, Leiko: dog

5. *Answers may vary. Sample:* The answers were different for each method. Dog was the most popular pet in 2 out of the 3 methods.

Explore It *Answers may vary. Sample:* In a random sample you randomly pick a given number of people from the population. In a convenience sample you pick people who are easy to ask. In a systematic sample you pick one person at random and then use a system to pick the other people in the survey. I think a random sample is the most fair because everyone has the same chance of being selected.

Probability and Replacement

When does the probability of an event change?
Solve these problems to find out.

1. Suppose you roll a 1–6 number cube. What is the probability of rolling the number 5 on the first roll? on the second roll? Explain.

_____

There are 3 red marbles and 4 blue marbles in a bag.
Use this information for Problems 2–5.

2. What is the probability of drawing a red marble from the bag? Explain.

_____

3. Suppose you draw a red marble on the first draw. Then you place the red marble back in the bag. What is the probability of drawing a red marble from the bag on your second draw? Explain.

_____

4. **Analyze** Suppose you draw a red marble on the first draw. You do NOT place the red marble back in the bag. What is the probability of drawing a red marble from the bag on your second draw? Explain.

_____

5. Suppose you draw a red marble on the first draw. Then you place the red marble back in the bag. What is the probability of drawing a blue marble from the bag on your second draw? Explain.

_____

Extend It

Explain when the probability of an event changes in an experiment.

Teacher Notes

Extend: Probability and Replacement

Objective Investigate probability with replacement and without replacement.

Using the Extend (Activities to use after Lesson 3)

In this activity, students are introduced to independent and dependent probability experiments. They investigate how probability changes when the sample space changes for the same experiment. In the Extend It, students are asked to draw possible conclusions about when the probability of an event might change in an experiment.

Math Journal You may wish to have students use their *Math Journals* to answer the Extend It activity.

Going Beyond You may wish to tell students that this activity introduces them to independent and dependent probability. Elicit that the probability changes when the conditions (of the sample space) change. Have students suggest experiments that would be affected by independent and dependent probability as well as those that would not. For example, contrast the probability of drawing cards from a deck and returning the cards to the deck versus removing them.

Solutions

1. $P(5) = \frac{1}{6}$ on each of the two rolls. *Answers may vary. Sample:* The favorable outcome is always one number, 5. The number of total possible outcomes is always 6.

2. $P(\text{red}) = \frac{3}{7}$. *Answers may vary. Sample:* There are 3 red marbles, the favorable outcome. There are 7 marbles in all.

3. $P(\text{red}) = \frac{3}{7}$. *Answers may vary. Sample:* There are 3 red marbles, the favorable outcome. There are 7 marbles in all.

4. $P(\text{red}) = \frac{2}{6} = \frac{1}{3}$. *Answers may vary. Sample:* Now there are 2 red marbles and 4 blue marbles in the bag. There are 2 red marbles, the favorable outcome. There are 6 marbles in all.

5. $P(\text{blue}) = \frac{4}{7}$. *Answers may vary. Sample:* There are 4 blue marbles, the favorable outcome. There are 7 marbles in all.

Extend It *Answers may vary. Sample:* The probability of an event does not change when the total number of possible outcomes and favorable outcomes does not change. The probability changes when the total number of possible outcomes and favorable outcomes change.

Card Experiment

In probability, an **event** is a possible outcome.

If you roll a 1–6 number cube, an event is "the cube lands on 2."

Another event is "the cube lands on an even number." The possible outcomes for this event are that the cube lands on 2, 4, or 6.

1. **Create** Use a deck of number cards. Design an experiment using the cards so that the probability of an event is greater than $\frac{1}{2}$. Explain your experiment.

_____

_____

2. What are all the possible outcomes in your experiment?

_____

3. **Analyze** What is the probability of the event you described in Exercise 1?

How do you know? _____

_____

4. What are all the possible outcomes that correspond to the event you described in Exercise 1? List the probability of each outcome.

_____

_____

Connect It

Look back at the probability of the event you described in Exercise 1. Compare this probability to the probability of all the outcomes that correspond to the event. Describe how they are related.

Teacher Notes

Connect: Card Experiment

Objective Use number cards to design an experiment.
Materials number cards with some cards repeated

Using the Connect (Activities to use after Lesson 5)

In this activity, students use cards to design an experiment given a probability requirement. They may design an experiment for a compound event. They list all possible outcomes and probabilities for the event. They may also explore the event as a combination of simple events. In the Connect It, students may be able to connect a compound event to the simple events that define the compound event.

Math Journal You may wish to have students use their *Math Journals* for the Connect It activity.

Going Beyond Have students describe two other possible events that might occur during the experiment they designed in Exercise 1. Then have them find the probability for each of these events.

Solutions

Answers may vary. Answers are given for the experiment described in the sample answer for Exercise 1.

1. *Answers may vary. Sample:*
   Use the following number cards:
   2, 2, 3, 3, 4, 4, 4, 5.
   Experiment: Draw a card from the deck. What is the probability of drawing a number greater than 2?

2. *Answers may vary. Sample:*
   Possible outcomes are 2, 3, 4, and 5.

3. *Answers may vary. Sample:*
   (number greater than 2) $= \frac{6}{8} = \frac{3}{4}$;
   There are 6 favorable outcomes:
   3, 3, 4, 4, 4, and 5; There are a total of 8 possible outcomes: 2, 2, 3, 3, 4, 4, 4, and 5.

4. *Answers may vary. Sample:*
   Possible favorable outcomes are 3, 4, and 5.
   Probability (3) $= \frac{2}{8} = \frac{1}{4}$,
   Probability (4) $= \frac{3}{8}$, and
   Probability (5) $= \frac{1}{8}$.

Connect It *Answers may vary. Sample:*
The probability of my event, drawing a number greater than 2, is $\frac{3}{4}$ which is greater than the probability of drawing a 2, 3, 4 or 5. $P(2) = \frac{1}{4}$, $P(3) = \frac{1}{4}$, $P(4) = \frac{3}{8}$, $P(5) = \frac{1}{8}$. The probability of all the events add up to 1.

Name _____ Date _____

Distances Between Points

There are many ways to move between points on a coordinate grid.

Way 1: You can move from point *A* to point *B* in 4 units.

Way 2: You also could move from point *A* to Point *B* in 6 units.

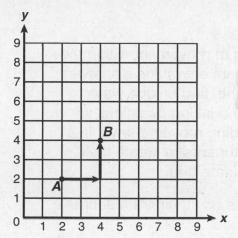

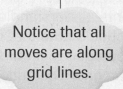

Notice that all moves are along grid lines.

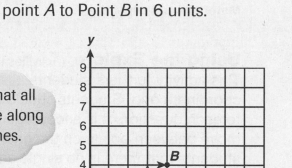

Move 2 units right, then move 2 units up. This is the shortest way to move between points *A* and *B*.

Move 1 unit down, then move 1 unit right, then move 3 units up, then move 1 unit right.

1. What other ways can you move from point *A* to point *B*:

in 4 units? _____

in 6 units? _____

2. Analyze Write 2 other ways that you can move from point *A* to point *B* using a different number of units. Do you notice a pattern? Explain.

_____

_____

_____

Explore It

Write problems about the distances between the points on the grid. Then explain how to solve your problems.

Teacher Notes

Explore: Distances Between Points

Objective Find distances between points on a coordinate grid.
Materials grid paper

Using the Explore (Activities to use after Lesson 1)

This activity furthers students' understanding of movement within the coordinate grid. Students should note that there are multiple answers to each question. It is encouraged that students find unique ways to move between points on the grid. The critical thinking questions show students that there is no single answer regarding movement within a coordinate grid. The Explore It encourages students to create their own questions using the points on the coordinate grid.

Math Journal You may wish to have students use their *Math Journals* for the Explore It activity.

Going Beyond Have students plot and label their own points on a coordinate grid. Then have them ask questions regarding the distances between points.

Solutions

1. *Answers may vary. Sample:*
   4 units: 1 unit up, 1 unit right, 1 unit up, 1 unit right.

   6 units: 3 units up, 2 units right, 1 unit down.

2. *Answers may vary. Sample:*
   8 units: 2 units down, 2 units right, 4 units up.

   10 units: 1 unit up, 1 unit left, 1 unit up, 1 unit left, 1 unit up, 4 units right, 1 unit down.

You can move only between points *A* and *B* using an even number of units.

Explore It *Answers may vary. Sample:*
Find and label three different points that are 4 units away from B.

B to C: 2 units up, 2 units left

B to D: 4 units up

B to E: 1 unit down, 2 units left, 1 unit up

Graphing Shapes

Sometimes you can graph a shape by knowing only a few ordered pairs.

Graph a square using the ordered pairs (1, 1) and (1, 3).

Step 1: Graph the ordered pairs.

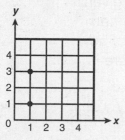

Step 2: Draw two more points to make a square. Then connect the points.

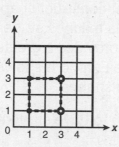

Think
(1, 1) and (1, 3) are 2 units apart, so all the ordered pairs must be 2 units apart to make a square.

1. List other shapes you can make using the ordered pairs (1, 1) and (1, 3). Then write the ordered pairs for each shape.

_____

Create the following shapes using the ordered pairs given as two of the vertices. Write the ordered pairs for each shape.

2. Trapezoid: (3, 5) (4, 5)

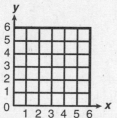

3. Hexagon: (1, 2) (4, 2)

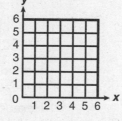

4. Octagon: (1, 4) (2, 5)

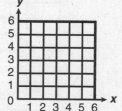

_____   _____   _____

_____   _____   _____

Extend It

Copy the grid above on a sheet of grid paper. Write another set of ordered pairs to make each of the shapes above. Use the ordered pairs given as two of the vertices. Use different ordered pairs to make the shapes.

Teacher Notes

Extend: Graphing Shapes

Objective Graph shapes on a coordinate grid given select ordered pairs.

Using the Extend (Activities to use after Lesson 3)

In this activity, students must construct shapes when they are given only a few ordered pairs. This teaches students how geometry and graphing are related. It also provides a greater understanding of how shapes are constructed. The Extend It shows students that there is more than one way to graph shapes.

Math Journal You may wish to have students use their *Math Journals* for the Extend It activity.

Going Beyond Have students create other shapes on a blank grid. Have them write the ordered pairs for the shapes they make.

Solutions

1. *Answers may vary. Sample:*
   Triangle: (1, 1) (1, 3) (3, 1)
   Rectangle: (1, 1) (1, 3) (4, 3) (4, 1)
   Parallelogram: (1, 1) (1, 3) (3, 4) (3, 2)

Answers may vary. Samples:

2.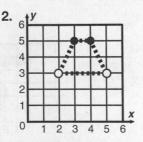

   (2, 3) (5, 3) (3, 5) (4, 5)

3.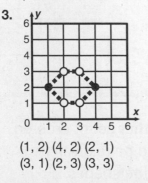

   (1, 2) (4, 2) (2, 1)
   (3, 1) (2, 3) (3, 3)

4.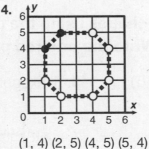

   (1, 4) (2, 5) (4, 5) (5, 4)
   (5, 2) (4, 1) (2, 1) (1, 2)

Extend It *Answers may vary. Samples:*
Trapezoid: (2, 4) (5, 4) (3, 5) (4, 5)

Hexagon: (1, 2) (4, 2) (5, 3) (0, 3)
(1, 4) (4, 4)

Octagon: (1, 4) (2, 5) (5, 5) (6, 4) (6, 2)
(5, 1) (2, 1) (1, 2)

Graph and Compare Functions

You can compare more than one function on the same grid!

Shea and Eva are selling crafts at a fair. Shea sold 5 crafts in the first hour, then sold 1 craft each hour after that. Eva sold 1 craft in the first hour, then sold 2 crafts each hour after that. Complete the tables.

Shea's Crafts	
Number of Hours	Number of Crafts Sold
1	———
———	6
3	7

Remember
Shea sold 5 crafts after 1 hour.
Eva sold 1 craft after 1 hour.

Eva's Crafts	
Number of Hours	Number of Crafts Sold
———	1
2	3
3	———

Make a line graph showing the number of crafts that Shea sold. Then make a line graph showing the number of crafts that Eva sold.

1. **Analyze** Extend the lines. When will Eva and Shea have sold the same number of crafts?

_____

2. **Predict** Will Eva ever sell more crafts than Shea? Explain why or why not.

_____

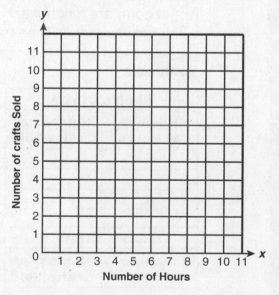

Connect It

Imagine you are also selling crafts at the fair. Make a table showing the number of crafts you sell each hour. Graph your table in the grid above. Then compare the number of crafts you sold each hour to the number of crafts Eva and Shea sold each hour. Describe your sales compared to Eva's sales and Shea's sales.

Teacher Notes

Connect: Graph and Compare Functions

Objective Graph more than one function and compare the functions at given points.

Using the Connect (Activities to use after Lesson 5)

Learning to compare functions is a useful and necessary skill. Students will receive an introduction to graphing and comparing functions. Students should notice that functions have varying values at different points. The critical thinking questions show students that the functions are equal or unequal at various points. The Connect It challenges students to compare 3 functions by creating their own unique function.

Math Journal You may wish to have students use their *Math Journals* for the Connect It activity.

Going Beyond Have students create a new scenario where they would compare functions. Have students create two function tables using their scenario. Then have them graph and compare the functions.

Solutions

Shea's Crafts

Number of Hours	Number of Crafts Sold
1	5
2	6
3	7

Eva's Crafts

Number of Hours	Number of Crafts Sold
1	1
2	3
3	5

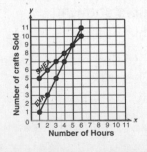

1. Eva and Shea both will have sold 9 crafts after 5 hours.

2. Yes, because after 6 hours, Eva will have sold 11 crafts, while Shea will have sold only 10 crafts. This is because Eva sells 2 crafts each hour, while Shea sells only 1 craft each hour.

Connect It *Answers may vary. Sample:* I sold no crafts the first hour, then 3 crafts each hour after that. I sold more crafts than both Eva and Shea after 4 hours.

My Crafts

Number of Hours	Number of Crafts Sold
1	0
2	3
3	6

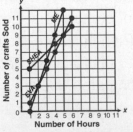